PIRATES

The Pirate's Pronunciation Handbook

Advanced Phonics, Spelling Skills & Cursive Writing Practice

ALEXANDRA BRETUSH & SARAH JANISSE BROWN

The Thinking Tree, LLC - www.FunSchoolingBooks.com
Copyright 2019 – Do Not Copy – Dyslexie Font
FunSchoolingBooks.com

**CREATIVE LANGUAGE ARTS
THIS COURSE COVERS:**

The English Alphabet
The Cursive Alphabet
Cursive Writing Practice
Creative Writing
Poetry
Comic Creation
Drawing
Science
Spelling
Crosswords
Consonants, Vowels & Their Sounds
Phonetic Letter Pronunciation
Parts of Speech
Silent B
Silent H
Letter Combination CH
Letter Combination GH
Letter Combination PH
Letter Combination QU
Letter Combination SS
Letter Combination TH
Letter Combination WH
Letter Combination WR
Sound [SH]
Sound [YU]
All Vowel Sounds
And more!

DYSLEXIA & ESL FRIENDLY!

HOW TO USE THIS BOOK:

Ahoy Matey!

This is a handbook for studying English grammar, spelling, and pronunciation.

You will learn how to pronounce each letter and the most common letter combinations. You'll also learn cursive and an introduction to parts of speech.

We use the International Phonetic Alphabet for pronunciation sounds.

Phonetic sounds will be listed in [ ].

If you need help with these symbols, you can look online, ask a parent, librarian, or teacher.

LEARNING TOOLS REQUIRED TO COMPLETE THIS COURSE:

Black pens and #2 pencils for writing

Colored pencils or gel pens

A dictionary (optional but helpful)

Books you are currently reading

Books about pirates

Arrrrrre you ready to splash in and learn?

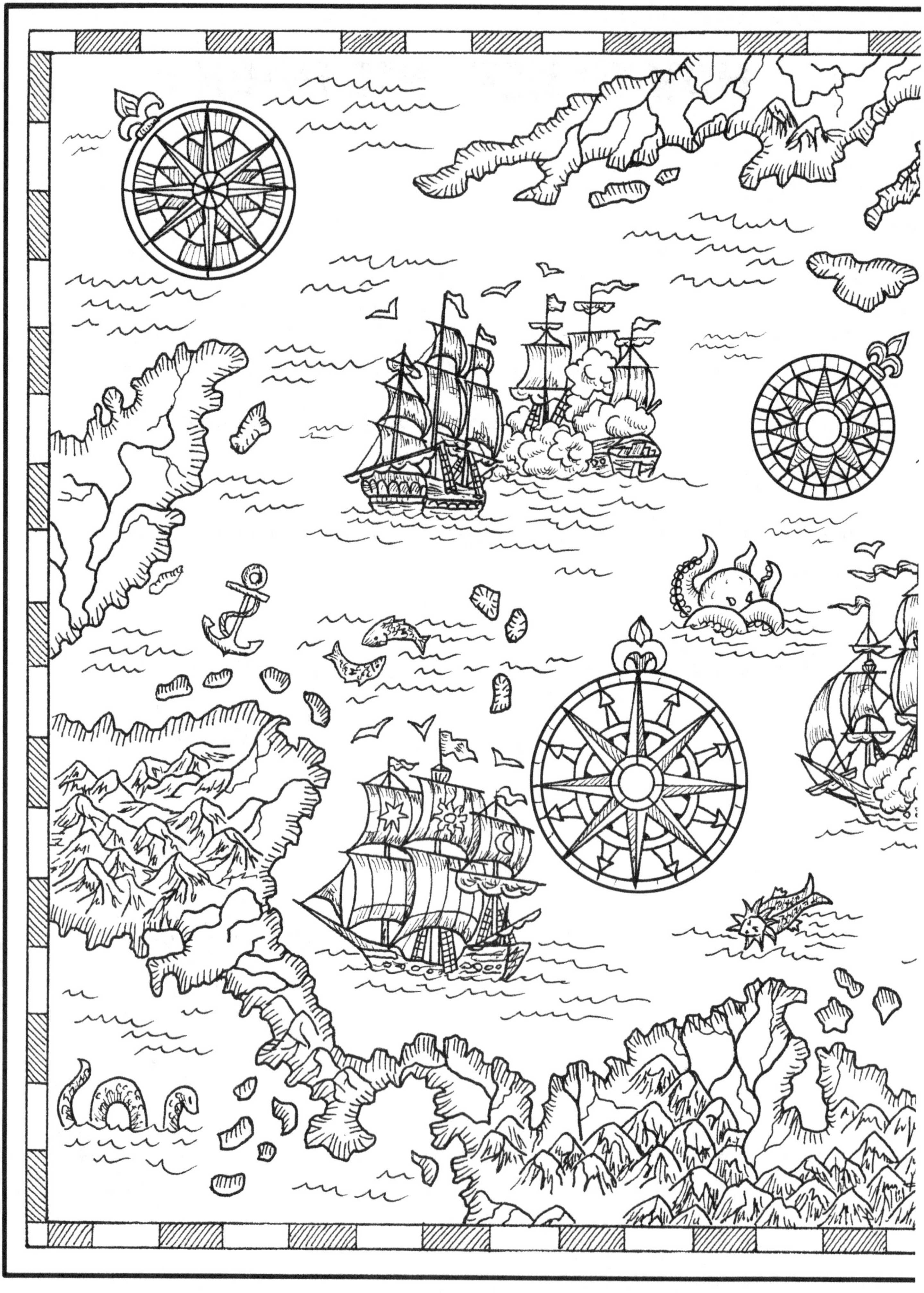

CARIBBEAN SEA MAP

English alphabet

How many letters are in the English alphabet? ____
Write them below in the correct order!

Trace the cursive alphabet

Aa Bb Cc Dd Ee Ff Gg
Hh Ii Jj Kk Ll Mm Nn
Oo Pp Qq Rr Ss Tt Uu
Vv Ww Xx Yy Zz

Practice writing cursive letters below

CONSONANTS

How many consonants are there in the English alphabet? ____

PRACTICE WRITING THE CONSONANTS IN CURSIVE

Aa Bb Cc Dd Ee Ff Gg
Hh Ii Jj Kk Ll Mm Nn
Oo Pp Qq Rr Ss Tt Uu
Vv Ww Xx Yy Zz

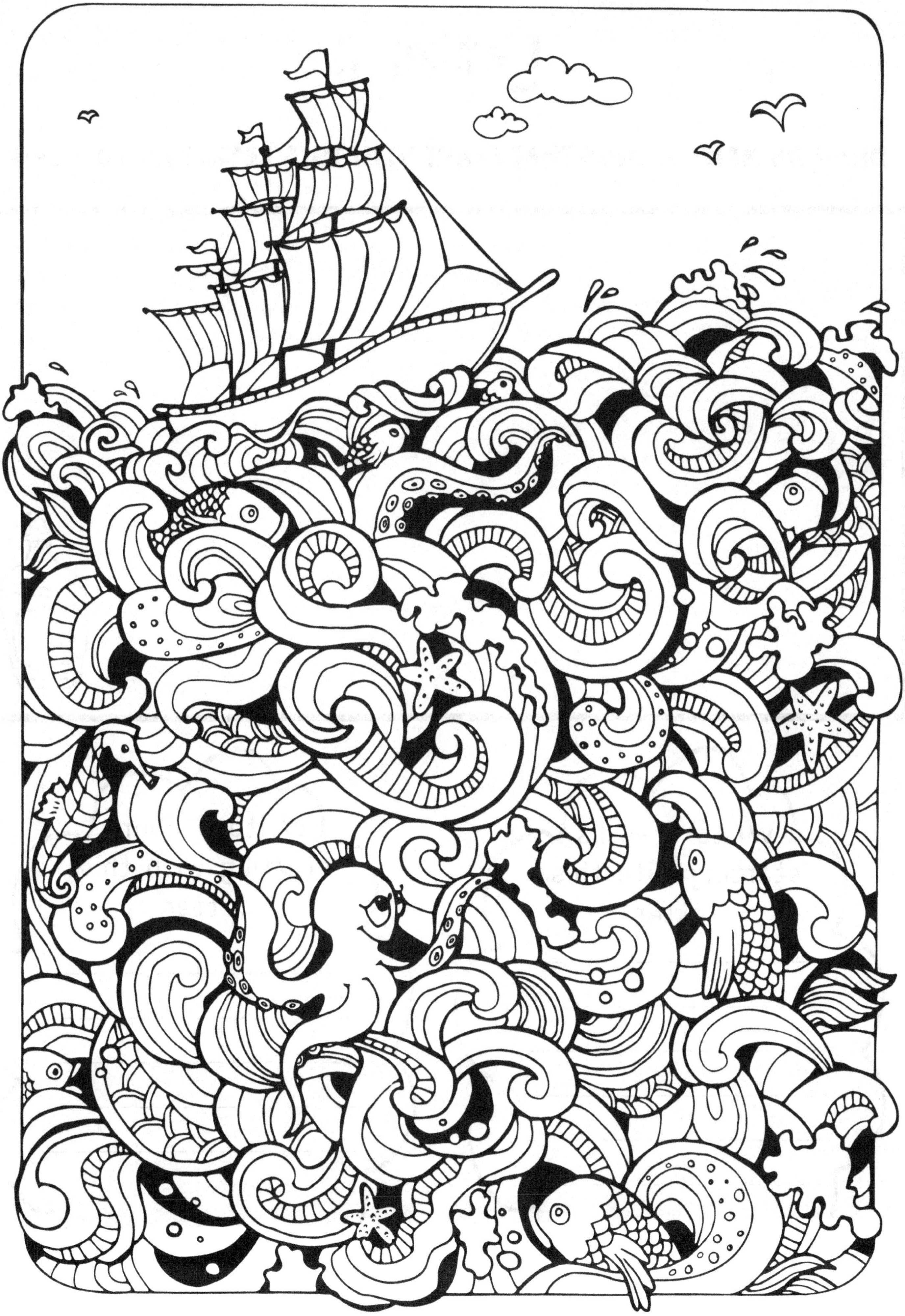

Letter B

DRAW AS MANY THINGS THAT START WITH THIS LETTER AS YOU CAN!

Write 6 verbs starting with this letter
_____
_____
_____
_____
_____
_____

Write 5 nouns starting with this letter
_____
_____
_____
_____
_____

Silent B

LETTER B CAN BE SILENT AT THE ENDS OF WORDS AFTER LETTER M

LAMB
COMB
BOMB
DUMB
WOMB

WRITE A SHORT STORY USING THE WORDS ABOVE:

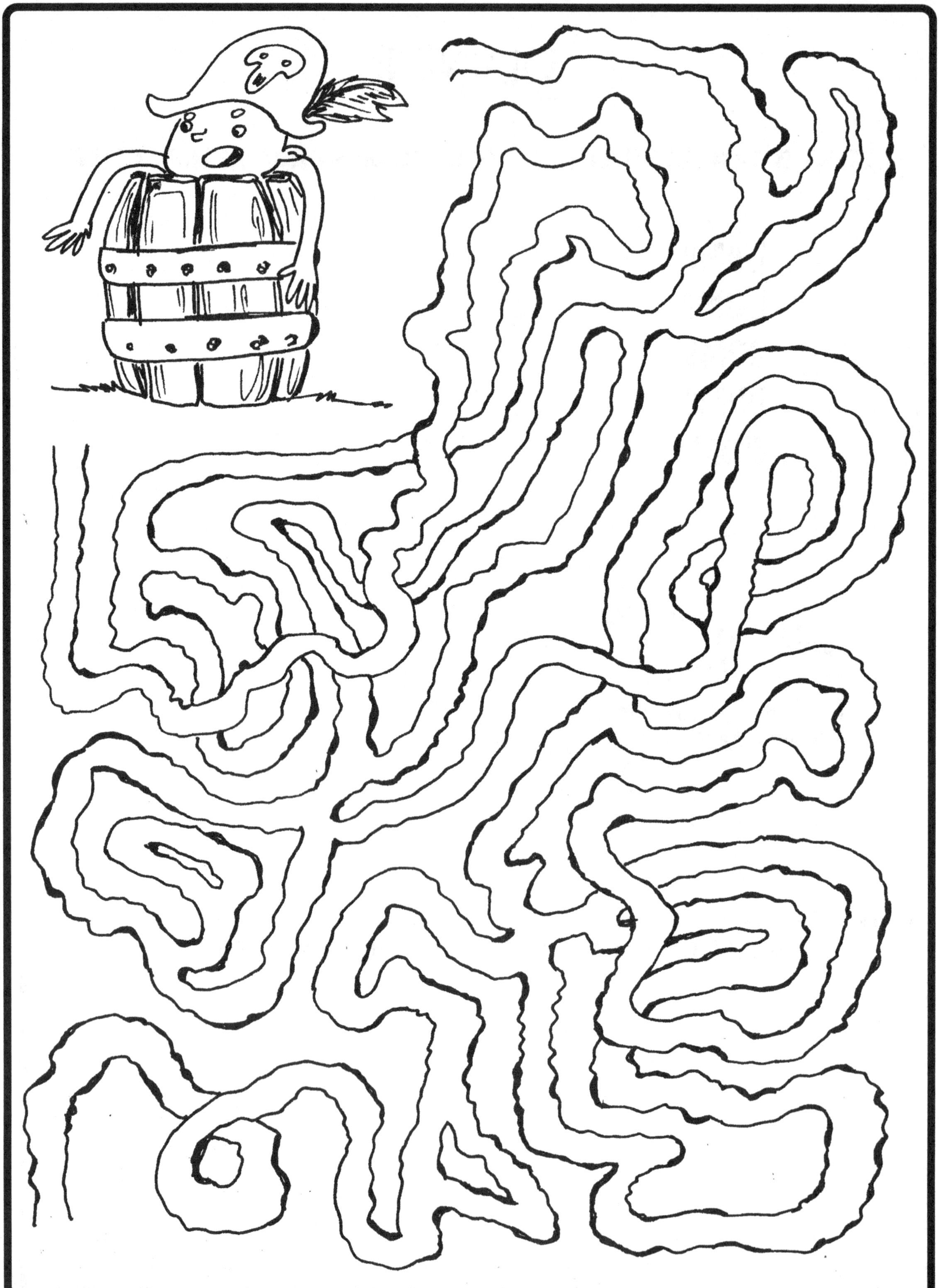

CURSIVE WRITING

Aa Bb Cc Dd Ee Ff Gg
Hh Ii Jj Kk Ll Mm Nn
Oo Pp Qq Rr Ss Tt Uu
Vv Ww Xx Yy Zz

Open the book you are reading at the moment. Find 10 words starting with this letter and write them in cursive below

_____   _____

_____   _____

_____   _____

_____   _____

_____   _____

Letter C

Fill in the blanks with words that begin with each sound.

Sound [S]

before the vowels

E, I, Y

CENTER
CIRCUS
CYCLE

_____
_____
_____
_____
_____
_____

Sound [K]

before the vowels

A, O, U

CAT
CORD
CUCUMBER

_____
_____
_____
_____
_____
_____

Sound [K]

before consonants

CLOWN
CROWD

_____

_____

_____

_____

WRITE A SHORT STORY OR POEM USING THE WORDS FROM THESE PAGES:

LETTER COMBINATION CH

Sound [CH]

Open one of the books on your reading list and write down as many words with this letter combination as you can

---

WRITE A SHORT STORY OR A POEM USING THESE WORDS:

LETTER COMBINATION CH

SOUND [K]

in words of Greek or Latin origin

CHAOS
CHEMISTRY
SCHOLAR
CHORUS

_____
_____
_____
_____

SOUND [SH]

in words of French origin

CHAMPAGNE
CHEF
CHANDALIER
MOUSTACHE

_____
_____
_____
_____

Date:

CURSIVE WRITING

Copy an interesting
paragraph from your pirate book in cursive

Book Title:_____ Page #_____

_____
_____
_____
_____
_____
_____
_____
_____
_____
_____

Aa Bb Cc Dd Ee Ff Gg
Hh Ii Jj Kk Ll Mm Nn
Oo Pp Qq Rr Ss Tt Uu
Vv Ww Xx Yy Zz

COMIC TIME

Create a Pirate Comic Strip

Letter D

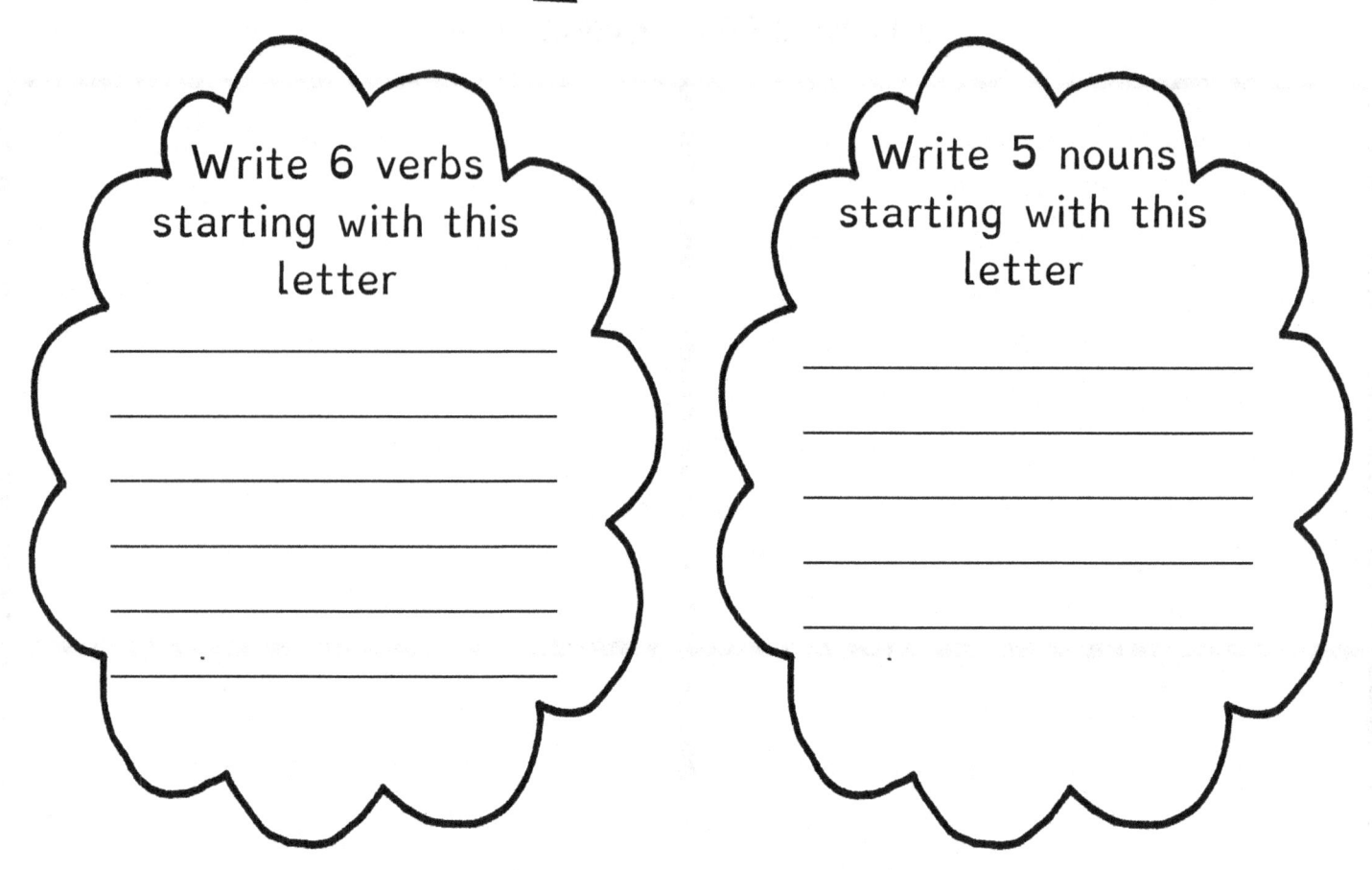

Write 6 verbs starting with this letter

_____
_____
_____
_____
_____
_____

Write 5 nouns starting with this letter

_____
_____
_____
_____
_____

WRITE A SHORT STORY USING THE WORDS ABOVE:

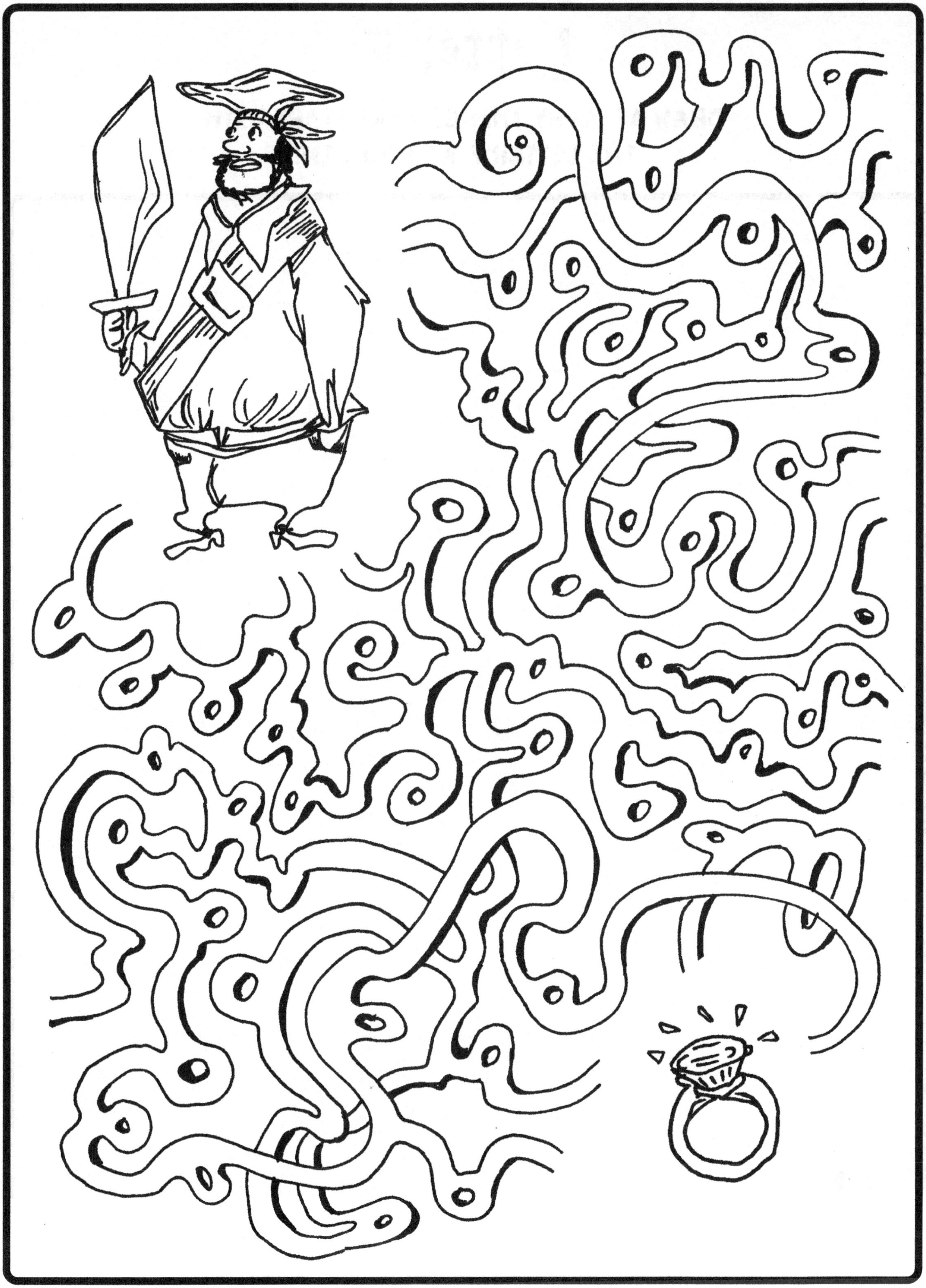

Letter F

DRAW AS MANY THINGS THAT START WITH THE LETTER F AS YOU CAN!

CURSIVE WRITING

Aa Bb Cc Dd Ee (Ff) Gg
Hh Ii Jj Kk Ll Mm Nn
Oo Pp Qq Rr Ss Tt Uu
Vv Ww Xx Yy Zz

Open the book you are reading at the moment. Find 10 words starting with this letter and write them in cursive below

_____   _____

_____   _____

_____   _____

_____   _____

_____   _____

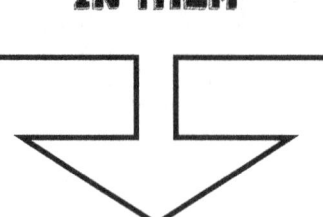

Letter G

FIRST WRITE AS MANY WORDS THAT YOU CAN WHICH HAVE LETTER G IN THEM

NEXT SORT THEM BY THE SOUND LETTER G MAKES ON THE NEXT PAGE

Morning, Sage _____
_____
_____
_____
_____

COLOR IN ONLY THE WORDS IN WHICH LETTER G MAKES THE SOUND [J]

AGENT   PAGE   GAP
   GUIDE
LEG   GAME
   GIANT
GREAT   GENERAL
   CAGE
         HUGE
ENERGY   EGG

SOUND [J]

Sage

_____
_____
_____
_____
_____
_____
_____
_____
_____
_____

SOUND [G]

Morning

_____
_____
_____
_____
_____
_____
_____
_____
_____
_____
_____

MAKE A FUNNY DRAWING ABOUT THE WORDS ABOVE

LETTER COMBINATION GH

Sound [G]
at the beginning of the word

GHOST
GHOUL

_____
_____
_____
_____
_____
_____

Sound [F]
At the end of some words

ENOUGH
LAUGH

_____
_____
_____
_____
_____
_____

USE THIS SPACE FOR FUNNY DRAWINGS AND DOODLES

IF GH COMES BEFORE T AT THE END OF THE WORD THE GH IS USUALLY SILENT!

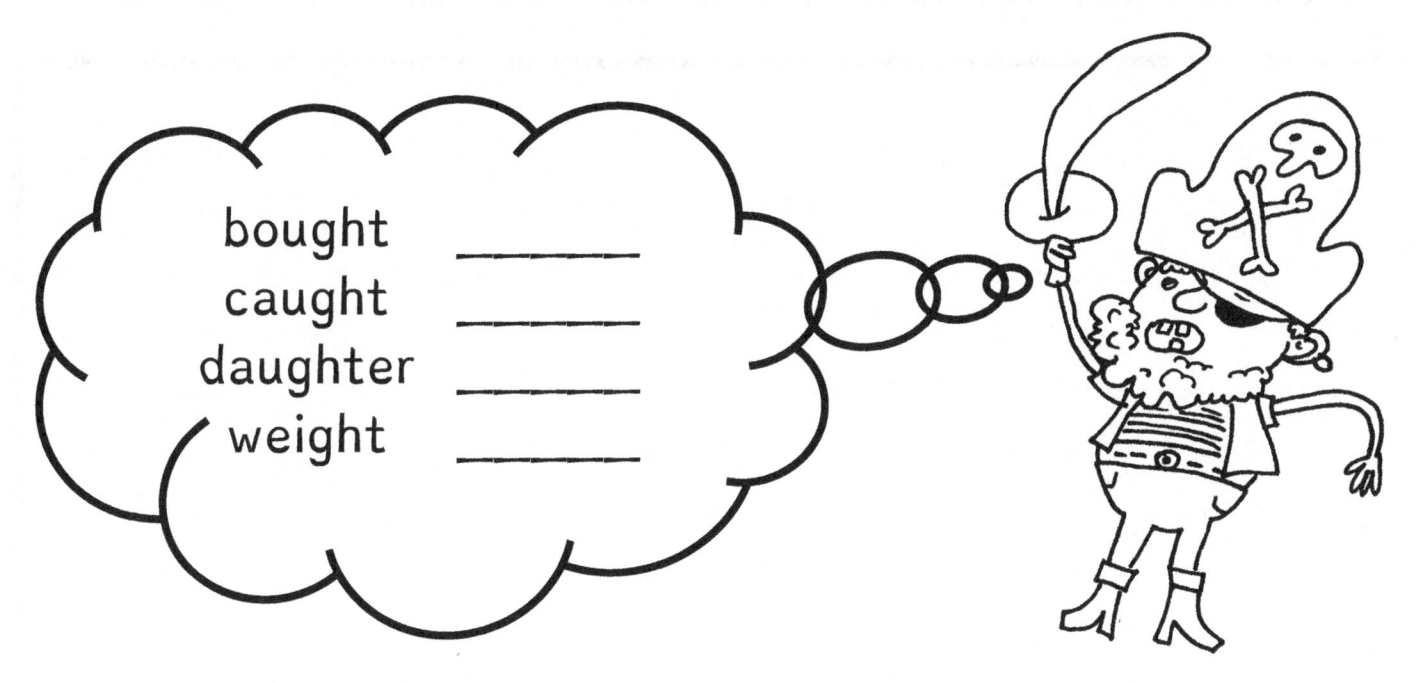

bought _____
caught _____
daughter _____
weight _____

MAKE A FUNNY POEM USING THE WORDS ABOVE

_____
_____
_____
_____
_____
_____
_____

Letter H

DRAW AS MANY THINGS THAT START WITH LETTER H AS YOU CAN!

Open the book you are reading at the moment. Find 10 words starting with this letter and write them below in cursive

_____   _____

_____   _____

_____   _____

_____   _____

_____   _____

Silent H

LETTER H CAN BE SILENT
WRITE A FEW WORDS WITH THE SILENT LETTER H!

Hour _____
_____ _____
_____ _____
_____ _____

Letter J

Aa Bb Cc Dd Ee Ff Gg
Hh Ii (Jj) Kk Ll Mm Nn
Oo Pp Qq Rr Ss Tt Uu
Vv Ww Xx Yy Zz

Open the book you are reading at the moment and find 10 words starting with this letter and write them below in cursive

_____   _____

_____   _____

_____   _____

_____   _____

_____   _____

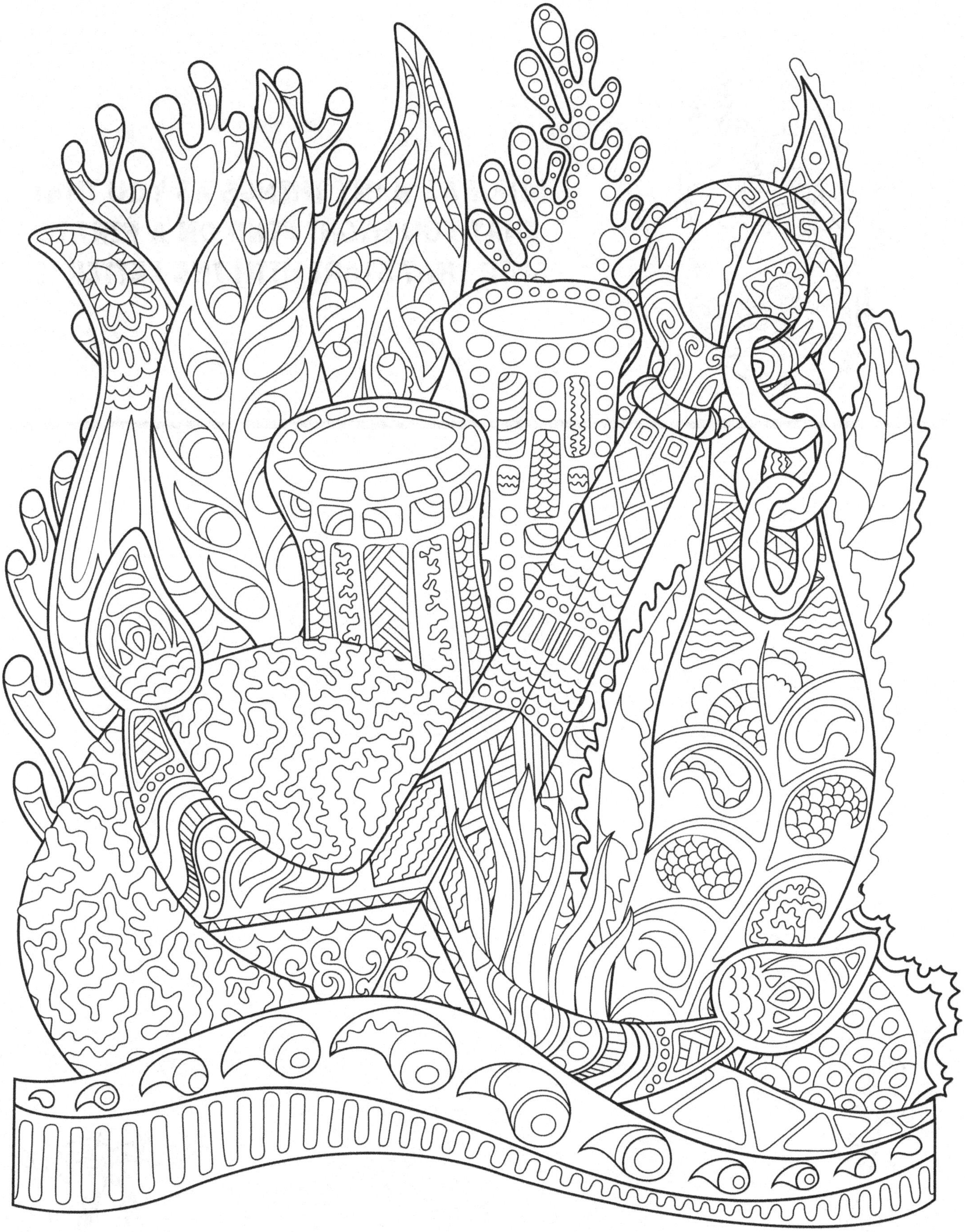

Letter K

DRAW AS MANY THINGS AS YOU THAT THAT YOU MIGHT FIND ON A PIRATE SHIP THAT START WITH THE LETTER K.

CREATIVE WRITING

Write 6 verbs starting with this letter
_____
_____
_____
_____
_____
_____

Write 5 nouns starting with this letter
_____
_____
_____
_____
_____

WRITE A SHORT STORY USING THE WORDS ABOVE:

CURSIVE WRITING

Write a pirate story in cursive:

_____
_____
_____
_____
_____
_____
_____
_____
_____
_____
_____
_____

Aa Bb Cc Dd Ee Ff Gg
Hh Ii Jj Kk Ll Mm Nn
Oo Pp Qq Rr Ss Tt Uu
Vv Ww Xx Yy Zz

COMIC TIME
Create a Pirate Comic Strip

Letter L

DRAW AS MANY THINGS THAT START WITH LETTER L THAT YOU CAN FIND UNDERWATER AS YOU CAN!

CREATIVE WRITING

Write 6 verbs starting with this letter
_____
_____
_____
_____
_____
_____

Write 5 nouns starting with this letter
_____
_____
_____
_____
_____

WRITE A SHORT STORY USING THE WORDS ABOVE:

Letter M

Write 6 nouns starting with this letter

Write 5 adjectives starting with this letter

WRITE A SHORT STORY USING THE WORDS ABOVE:

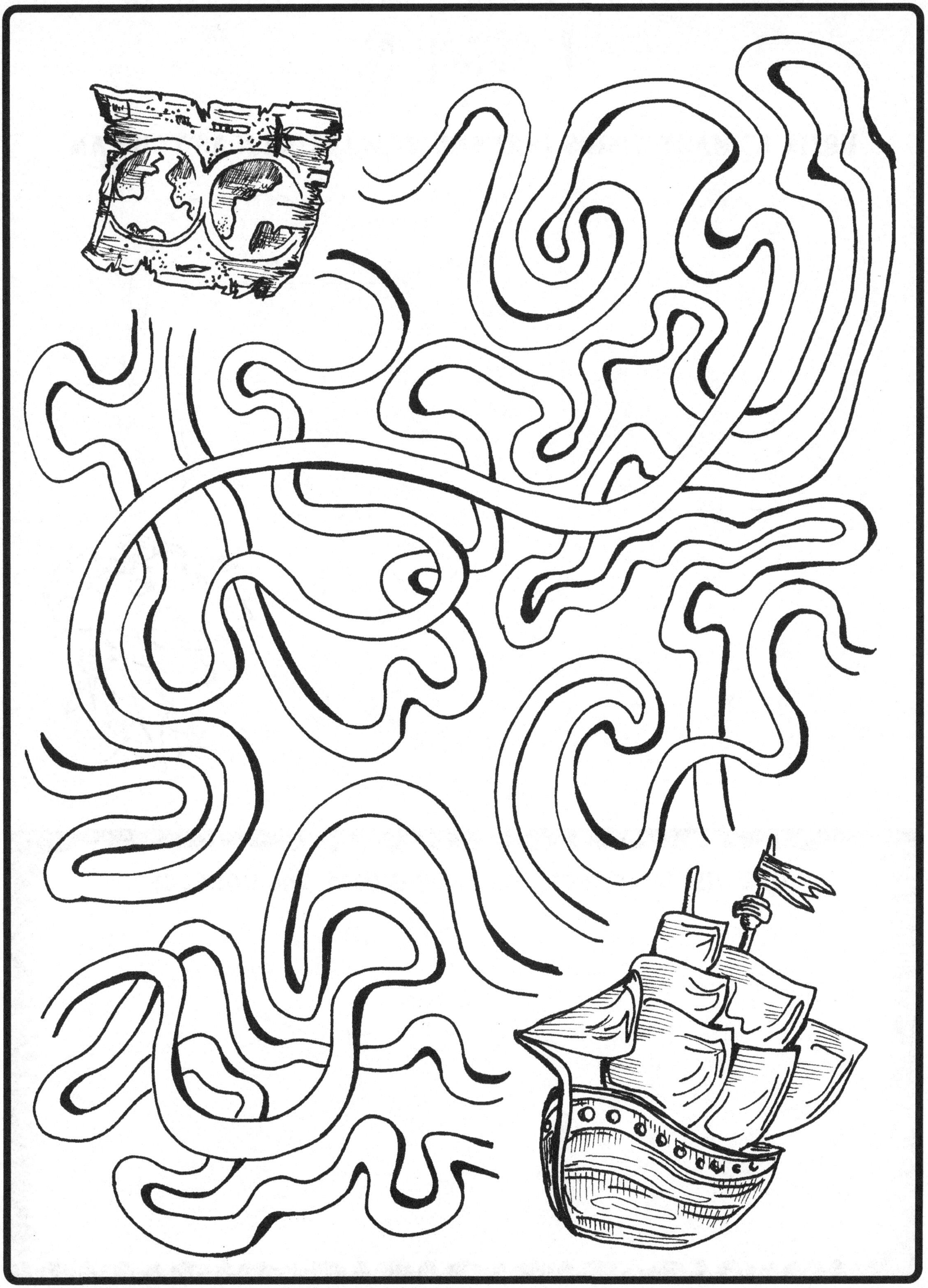

Letter N

WRITE AS MANY WORDS THAT END WITH LETTER N AS YOU CAN

USE THIS SPACE FOR FUNNY DRAWINGS AND DOODLES

Date: _____

COMIC TIME
Create a Pirate Comic Strip

Letter P

DRAW AS MANY THINGS THAT START WITH LETTER P AS YOU CAN!

Open the book you are reading at the moment. Find 10 words starting with this letter and write them below in cursive

Letter Combination PH
Sound [F]

PHONE
PHOTO
DOLPHIN
PHYSICS

MAKE AS MANY WORDS OUT OF THE WORD

PHOTOGRAPHY

AS YOU CAN

TROPHY

COLOR ME !

MAKE AS MANY WORDS OUT OF THE WORD
PIRATE
AS YOU CAN

AIR

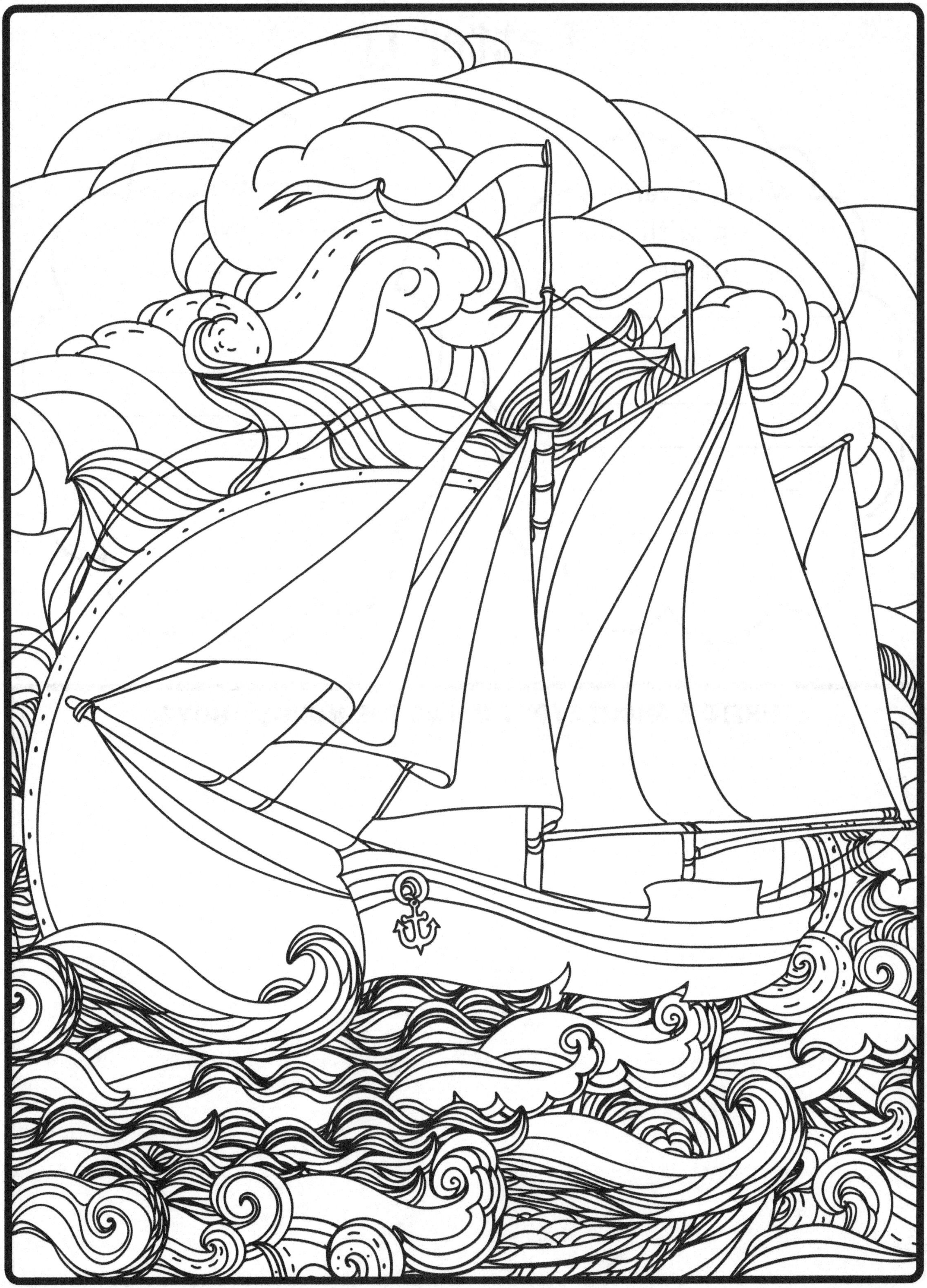

Letter Q

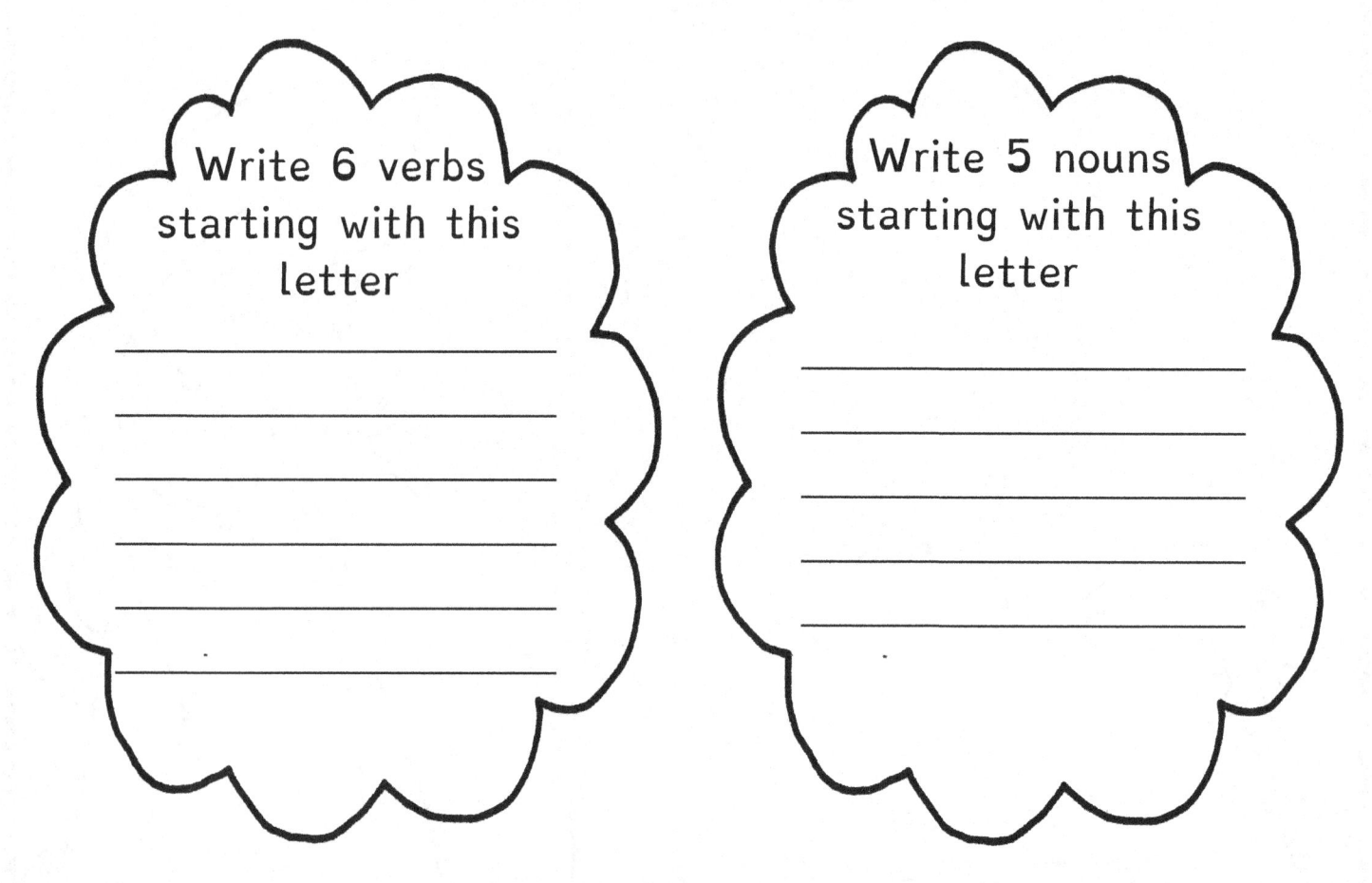

Write 6 verbs starting with this letter

Write 5 nouns starting with this letter

WRITE A SHORT STORY USING THE WORDS ABOVE:

LETTER COMBINATION QU

SOUND [K]

UNIQUE TECHNIQUE

_____
_____
_____
_____
_____
_____

SOUND [KW]

QUESTION QUEEN

_____
_____
_____
_____
_____
_____

WRITE A SHORT FUNNY POEM USING THE WORDS FROM THESE PAGES

Letter R

DRAW AS MANY THINGS THAT START WITH LETTER R AS YOU CAN!

CREATIVE WRITING

Write 6 verbs starting with this letter

_____
_____
_____
_____
_____
_____

Write 5 nouns starting with this letter

_____
_____
_____
_____
_____

WRITE A SHORT STORY USING THE WORDS ABOVE:

Letter S

Aa Bb Cc Dd Ee Ff Gg
Hh Ii Jj Kk Ll Mm Nn
Oo Pp Qq Rr Ss Tt Uu
Vv Ww Xx Yy Zz

Open the book you are reading at the moment. Find 10 words starting with this letter and write them below in cursive

_____   _____
_____   _____
_____   _____
_____   _____
_____   _____

TRACE AND COLOR ME!

WHAT IS MY NAME?

_____

Letter S
SOUND [S] OR SOUND [Z]

COLOR IN ONLY THE WORDS IN WHICH LETTER S MAKES SOUND {Z}

REASON   WAS   SEND

PRESENT   IS   ADVISE

CAUSE   BOYS

BUSY   WISE   EGGS

ALWAYS   STORY

CATS   THIS   KISS

STORM   SMELL

TUESDAY   SUNDAY

ROSE   MISTY   NOSE

Make up a Funny Story using the Words you colored in
Title:

_____

MAKE AN ILLUSTRATION FOR THIS STORY

Letter combination SS

lesson, loss, mass, mattress, mess, message

MAKE AS MANY WORDS OUT OF THE WORD

"PIRATESS" (Lady Pirate!)

AS YOU CAN

RAT

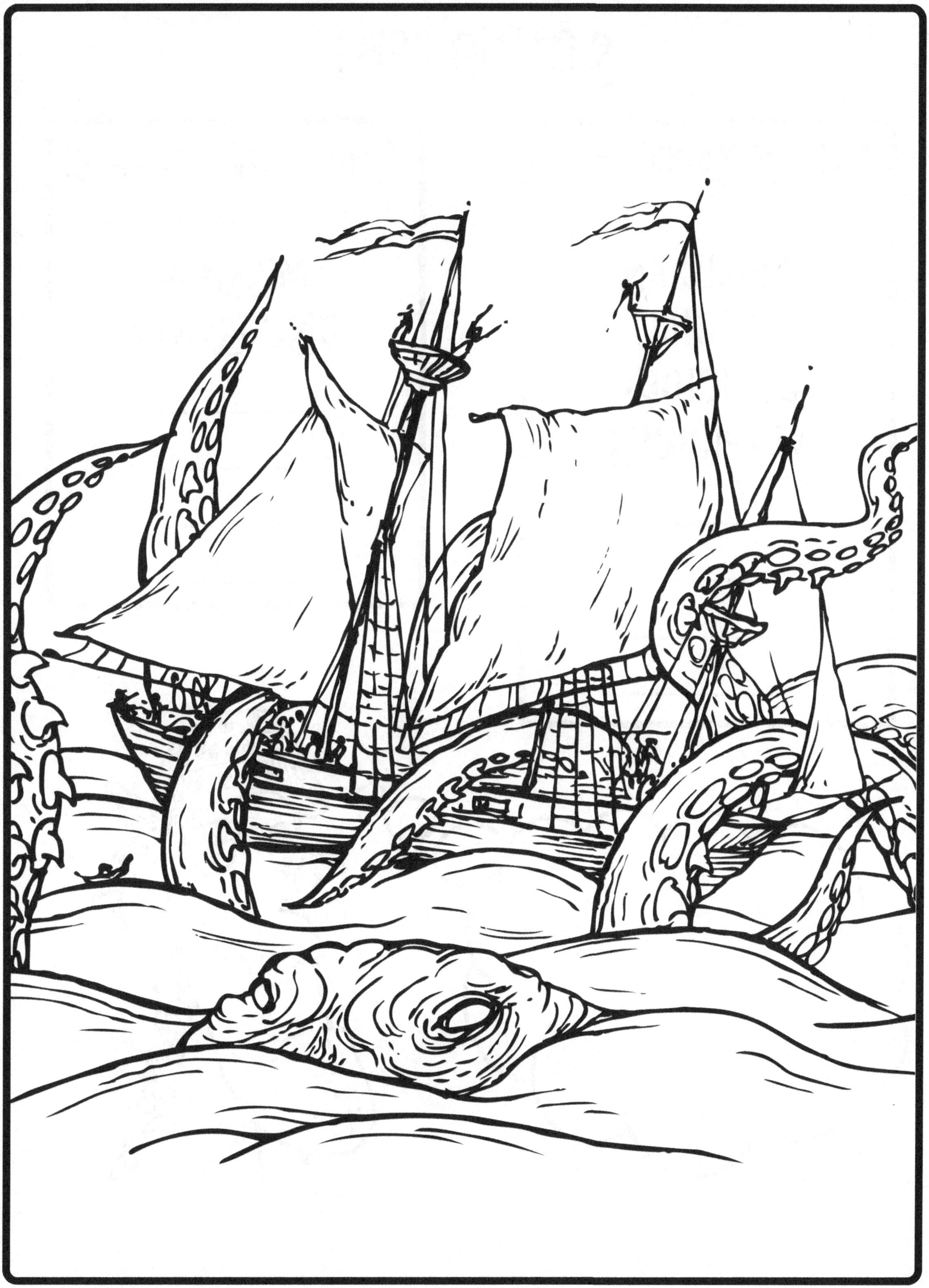

SOUND [SH]

The combination CI:

MUSICIAN
SPECIAL
DELICIOUS
SUSPICIOUS

____
____
____
____

The combination SI:

MISSION
DISCUSSION

____
____
____
____

SOUND [SH]

The combination TI:

PATIENT
CONDITION
AMBITIOUS

___
___
___
___

The combination SU:

SUGAR
PRESSURE
ISSUE

___
___
___
___

WRITE THREE FUNNY SENTENCES USING THE WORDS FROM THESE PAGES

1. _____
   _____

2. _____
   _____

3. _____
   _____

Letter T

DRAW AS MANY THINGS THAT START WITH LETTER T AS YOU CAN!

MAKE AS MANY WORDS OUT OF THE WORD

TREASURE

___Sea___ _____ _____ _____

_____ _____ _____ _____

_____ _____ _____ _____

_____ _____ _____ _____

_____ _____ _____ _____

CURSIVE WRITING

Aa Bb Cc Dd Ee Ff Gg
Hh Ii Jj Kk Ll Mm Nn
Oo Pp Qq Rr Ss (Tt) Uu
Vv Ww Xx Yy Zz

Open the book you are reading at the moment. Find 10 words starting with this letter and write them in cursive below

_____   _____

_____   _____

_____   _____

_____   _____

_____   _____

LETTER COMBINATION - TH

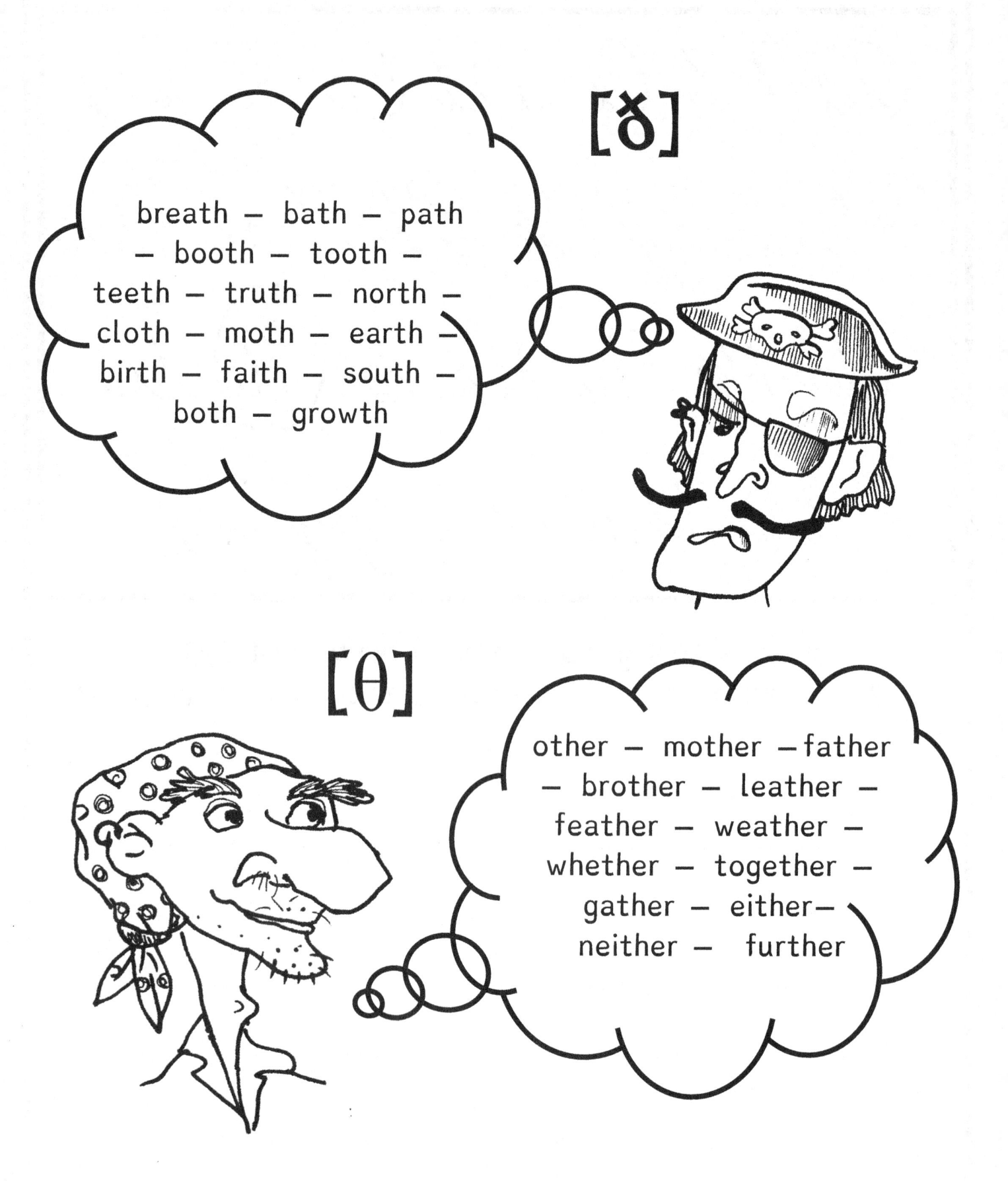

[ð]

breath – bath – path – booth – tooth – teeth – truth – north – cloth – moth – earth – birth – faith – south – both – growth

[θ]

other – mother – father – brother – leather – feather – weather – whether – together – gather – either – neither – further

Open the book you are reading at the moment and write below as many words with TH as you can. Then sort them below by the sound they make.

[ð]

[θ]

Date:
_____

READING TIME

Date: _____

Write a message in each bottle using words from your books.

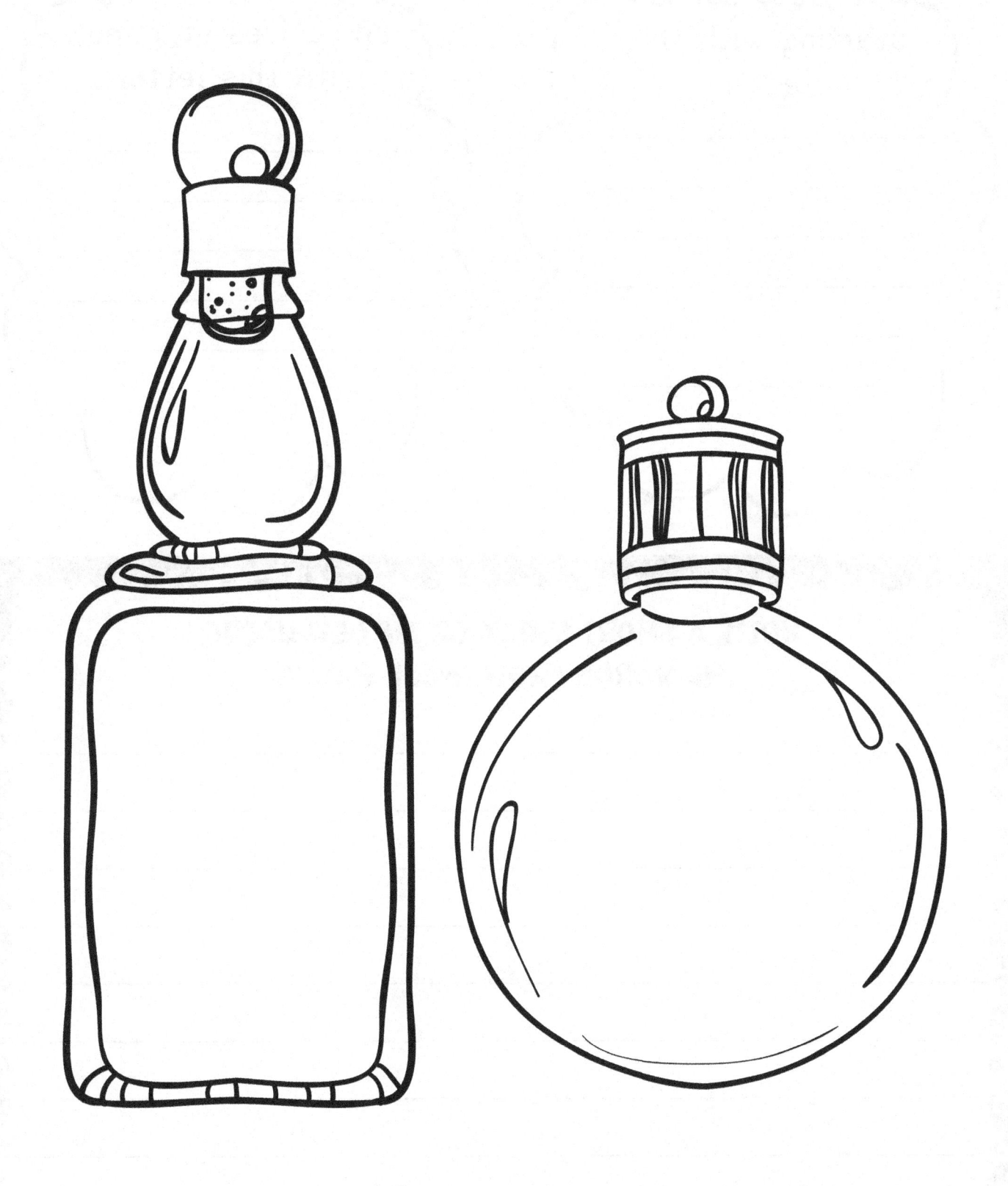

Letter V

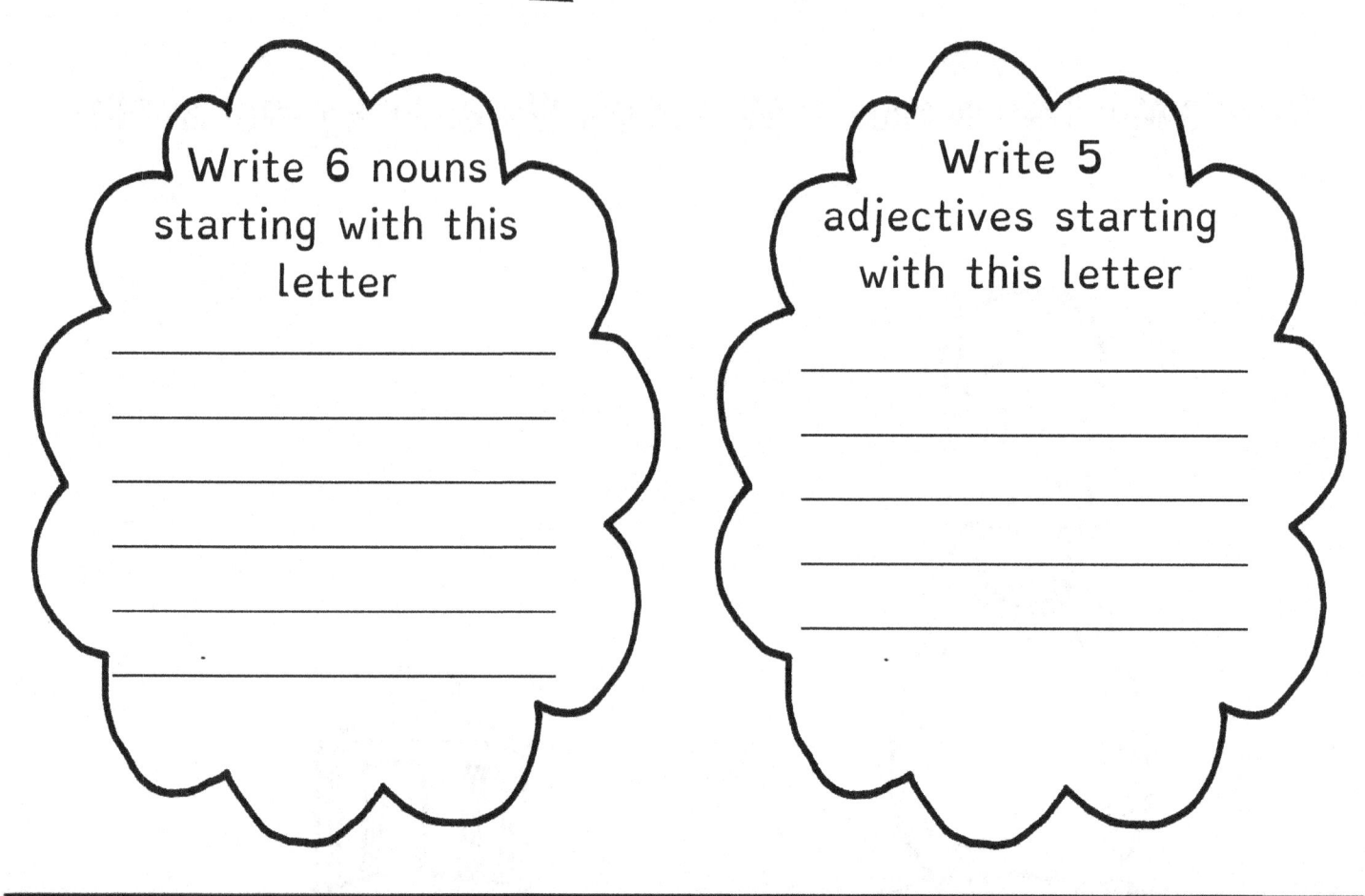

Write 6 nouns starting with this letter

Write 5 adjectives starting with this letter

WRITE A SHORT STORY OR A POEM USING THE WORDS FROM THESE PAGES:

Cursive Writing

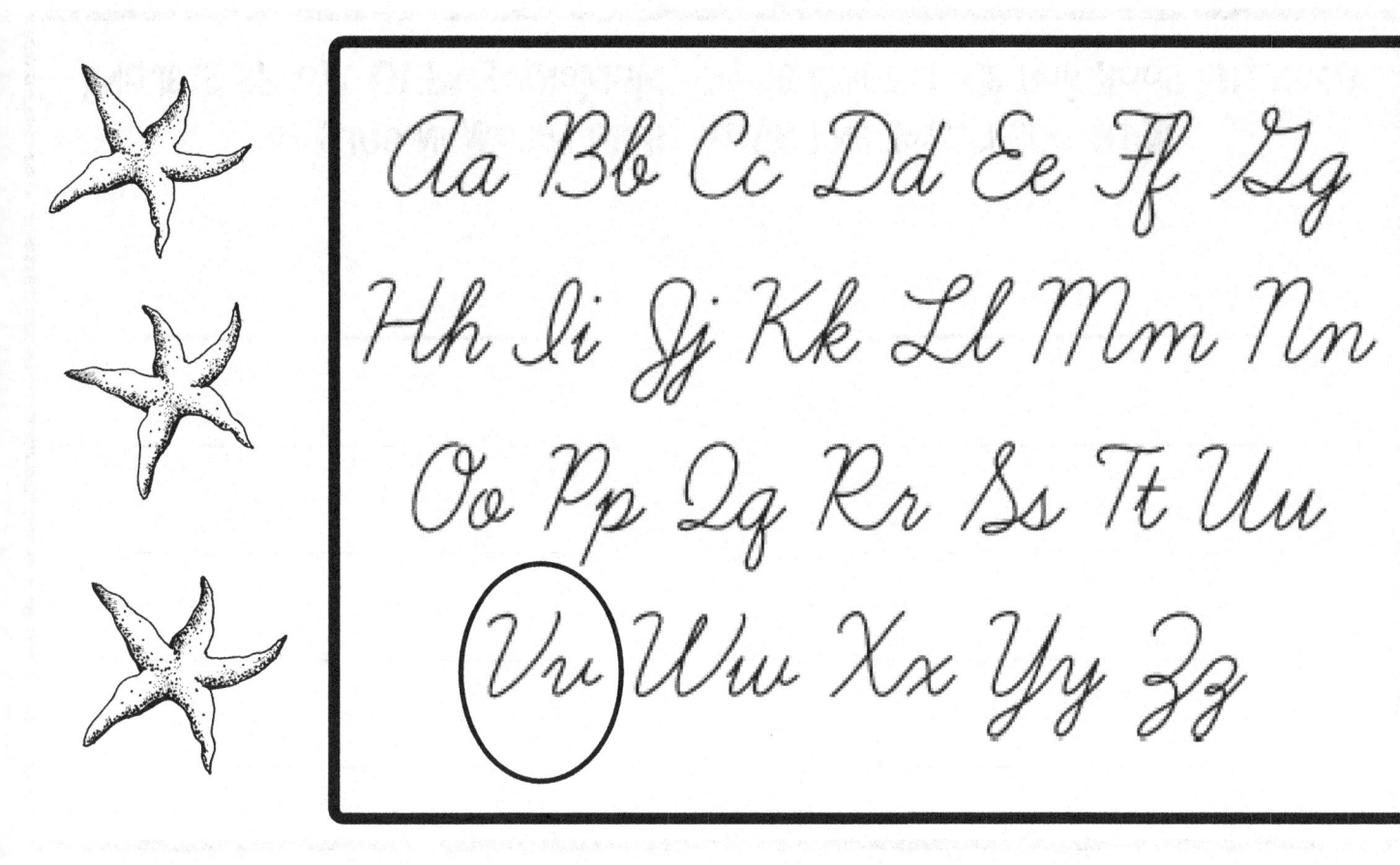

Aa Bb Cc Dd Ee Ff Gg
Hh Ii Jj Kk Ll Mm Nn
Oo Pp Qq Rr Ss Tt Uu
(Vv) Ww Xx Yy Zz

Open the book you are reading at the moment. Find 10 words starting with this letter and write them below in cursive

Letter W

Open the book you are reading at the moment. Find 10 words starting with this letter and write them below in cursive

_____   _____
_____   _____
_____   _____
_____   _____
_____   _____

WRITE A SHORT FUNNY POEM USING THE WORDS FROM THESE PAGES

LETTER COMBINATION Wh

WHAT	WHALE
WHOLE	WHEEL
WHERE	WHOSE
WHICH	WHEN
WHO	WHITE
WHOM	WHICH

SORT THE WORDS ABOVE BY THE SOUND THEY MAKE

Sound [W]

WHAT

_____
_____
_____
_____
_____
_____
_____

Sound [H]

WHOLE

_____
_____
_____
_____
_____
_____
_____

LETTER COMBINATION Wr

LETTER W CAN BE SILENT IN WR LETTER COMBINATION

Wreck _____
Wrist _____
Wrong _____
Write _____
Wrinkle _____
Wrap _____

WRITE A SHORT STORY USING THE WORDS ABOVE:

COMIC TIME
Create a Pirate Comic Strip

Letter X

DRAW AS MANY THINGS THAT START OR END WITH THE LETTER X AS YOU CAN!

CREATIVE WRITING

Write 6 verbs starting with this letter
_____
_____
_____
_____
_____
_____

Write 5 nouns starting with this letter
_____
_____
_____
_____
_____

WRITE A SHORT STORY USING THE WORDS ABOVE:

Letter X

SOUND [KS] OR SOUND [gz]

COLOR IN ONLY THE WORDS IN WHICH LETTER X MAKES THE SOUND {GZ}

- FIX
- EXAM
- EXIT
- RELAX
- EXPERIENCE
- EXAMPLE
- EXIST
- BOX
- EXOTIC
- EXTRACT
- MAXIMUM
- EXPECT
- EXPENSIVE
- EXHAUSTING
- EXACT
- EXPERIMENT
- EXILE
- ANXIETY
- AXIS
- EXCEPT

MAKE AS MANY WORDS OUT OF THE WORD
EXPERIENCE
AS YOU CAN

RICE

MAKE FUNNY ILLUSTRATIONS ABOUT THESE WORDS BELOW

Letter Y

DRAW AS MANY THINGS THAT START OR END WITH THE LETTER Y AS YOU CAN!

COLOR IN THE PICTURES AND FINISH THE WORDS WITH THIS LETTER

Y

Y

CURSIVE WRITING

Aa Bb Cc Dd Ee Ff Gg
Hh Ii Jj Kk Ll Mm Nn
Oo Pp Qq Rr Ss Tt Uu
Vv Ww Xx (Yy) Zz

Open the book you are reading at the moment. Find 10 words starting with this letter and write them in cursive below

_____   _____

_____   _____

_____   _____

_____   _____

_____   _____

Sound [yu:]

Letter Combinations EW	Letter U	Letter Combinations UE, UE
FEW	USE	DUE
DEW	USUAL	PURSUE
NEPHEW	HUMAN	SUIT
NEW	HUMOR	NEUTRAL
	REFUSE	

___
___
___

___
___
___
___

___
___
___
___

MAKE SOME DRAWINGS ABOUT THE WORDS ABOVE

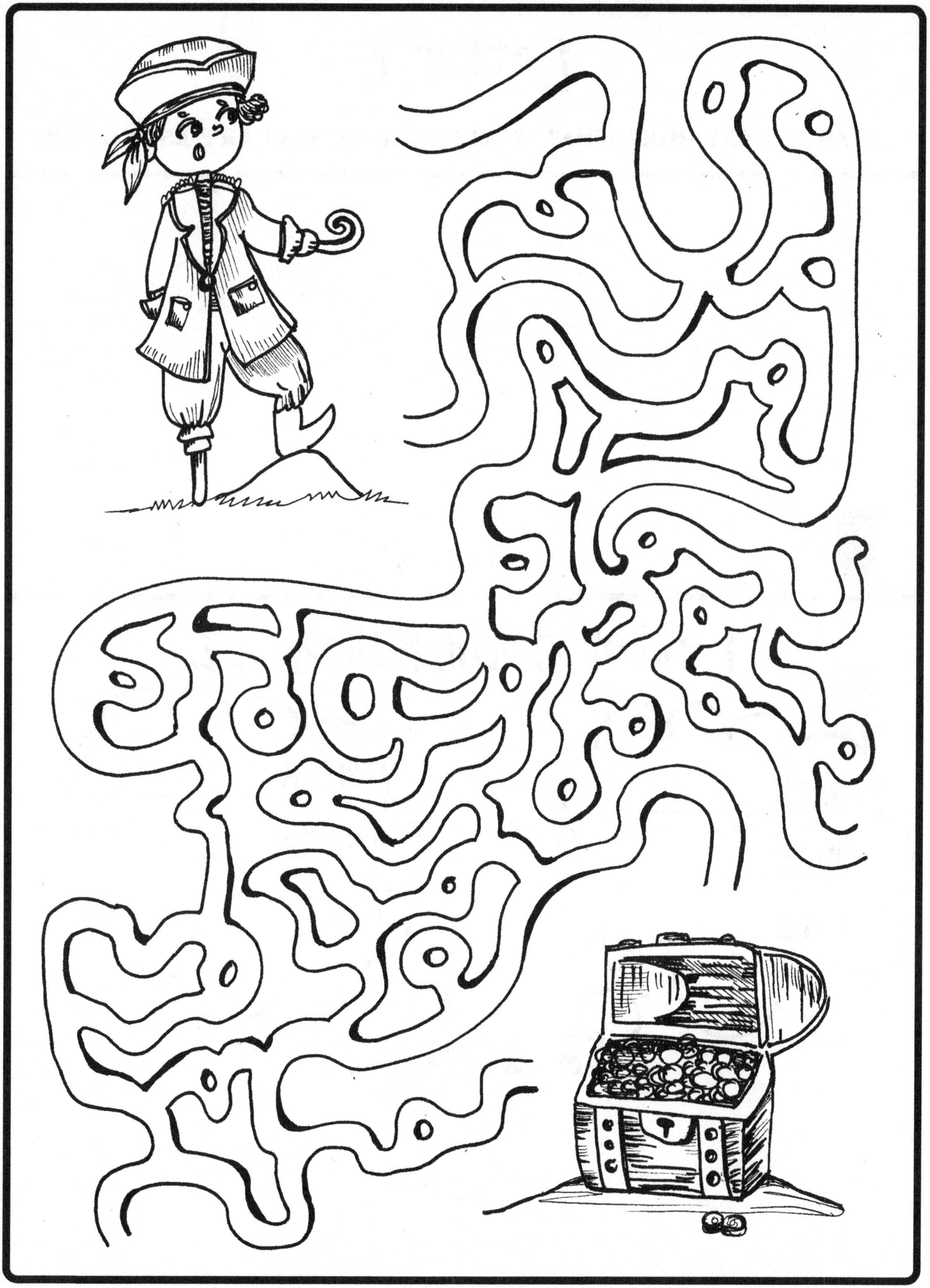

Letter Z

DRAW AS MANY THINGS THAT START OR END WITH LETTER Z AS YOU CAN!

Letter Combination ZZ

JAZZ _____

BUZZ _____

FUZZ _____

PIZZA _____

PUZZLE _____

DRIZZLE _____

CREATIVE WRITING

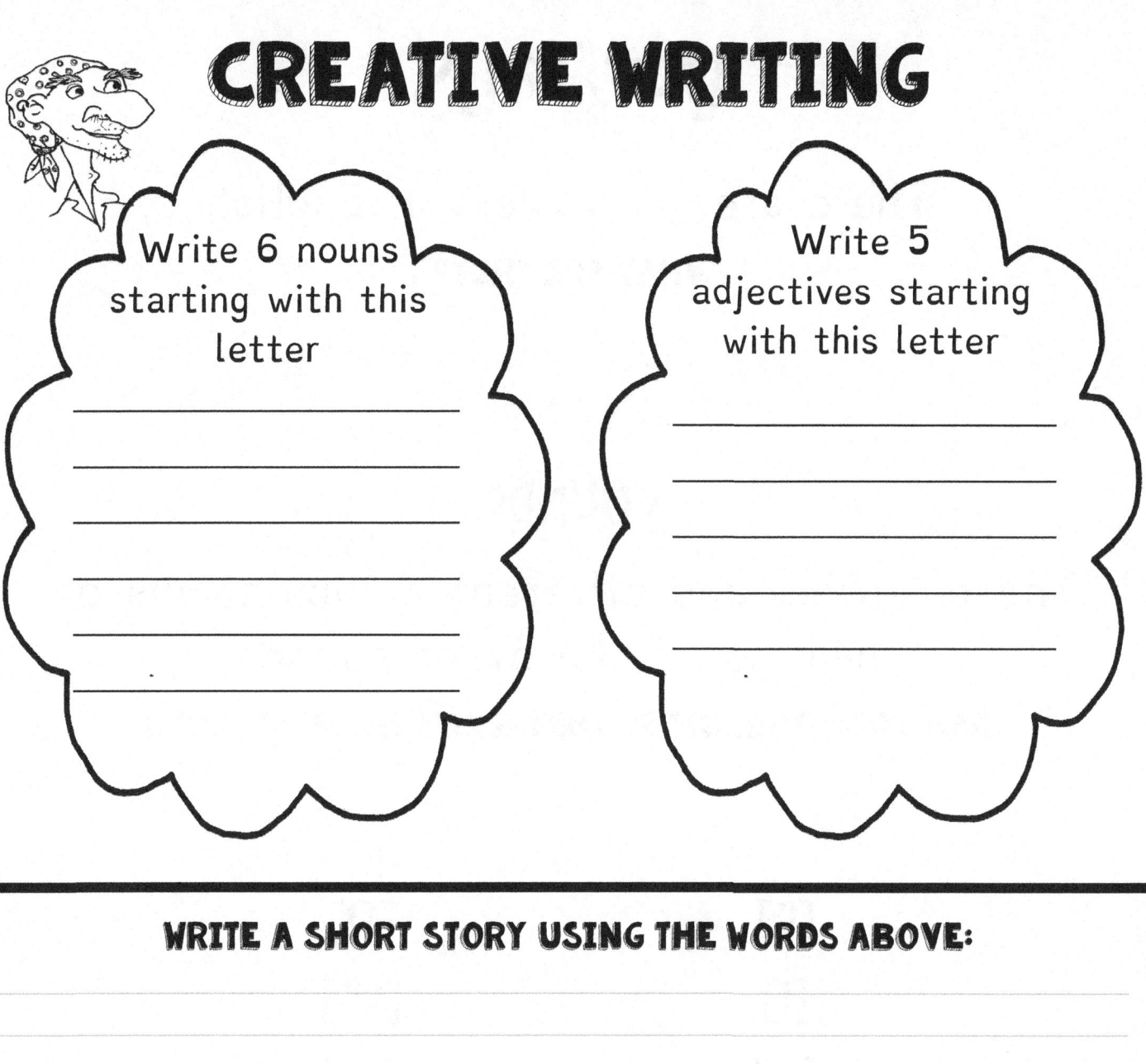

Write 6 nouns starting with this letter
_____
_____
_____
_____
_____
_____

Write 5 adjectives starting with this letter
_____
_____
_____
_____
_____

WRITE A SHORT STORY USING THE WORDS ABOVE:

VOWELS

There are six vowels in English

WHAT ARE THEY?

_____ _____ _____ _____ _____ _____

SOUNDS

These vowels and different combinations of them can make other sounds

ASK YOUR PARENTS IF THEY KNOW THESE SOUNDS!

[i:]	[o]
[i]	[o:]
[e]	[oi]
[ei]	[ou]
[i:]	[u]
[æ]	[u:]
[a]	[yu]
[ai]	[ə]
[au]	[ər]

Find and Color in Vowels Only!

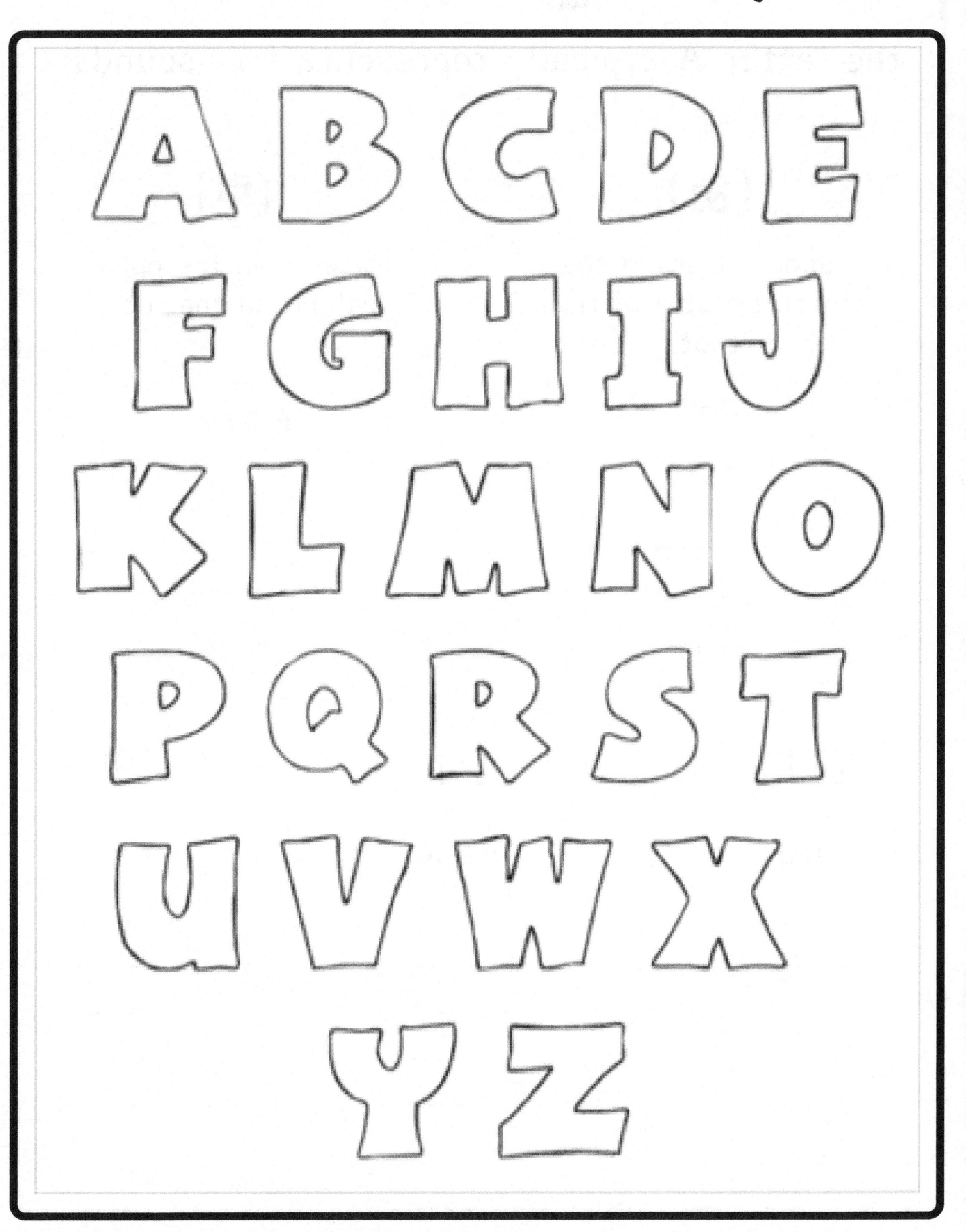

A B C D E

F G H I J

K L M N O

P Q R S T

U V W X

Y Z

Letter A

the letter A typically represents five sounds:

[æ]
under stress in the closed syllable of the root

hat

rat

_____

_____

_____

[ei]
letter A in the open syllable in the root

Kate

_____

_____

_____

[a:]

card

_____
_____
_____
_____

[ə]

alone

_____
_____
_____
_____

[O:]

call

_____
_____
_____
_____

A

DRAW AS MANY THINGS THAT START WITH LETTER A AS YOU CAN!

A

CREATIVE WRITING

A

Write 6 verbs starting with this letter

_____
_____
_____
_____
_____
_____

Write 5 nouns starting with this letter

_____
_____
_____
_____
_____

WRITE A SHORT STORY USING THE WORDS ABOVE:

A

[a:]
In British English, the letter A is pronounced [a:] before the consonants f, ff, ph, sk, sp, ss, st, th, nce, nd, and some others.

[æ]
In American English, the letter A under stress in the closed syllable of the root is usually pronounced [æ]

USE THIS SPACE FOR FUNNY DRAWINGS AND DOODLES

TRY SAYING THESE WORDS WITH BRITISH AND AMERICAN ACCENTS

staff, after, draft, half, ask, task, grasp, grass, glass, class, fast, last, castle, master

disaster, bath, path, example, chance, dance, answer, can't, demand, command

Sound [æ]

Letter A in the closed syllable—

Add more to the list and then put in alphabetical order

ASK	_____
Task	_____
Fast	_____
Last	_____
Master	_____
Castle	_____
Answer	_____
Act	_____
Pack	_____
Sand	_____
Class	_____
Glass	_____
_____	_____
_____	_____
_____	_____
_____	_____

COLOR IN THE PICTURES AND FINISH THE WORDS

Sound [aː]

Letter A
in some English words and words of foreign origin

PSALM
BALM
DRAMA
BRAVO

_____
_____
_____
_____
_____
_____

Letter combinations AR
in the root usually under stress

ART
CARD
PART
GUARD

_____
_____
_____
_____
_____
_____

CURSIVE WRITING

Aa Bb Cc Dd Ee Ff Gg
Hh Ii Jj Kk Ll Mm Nn
Oo Pp Qq Rr Ss Tt Uu
Vv Ww Xx Yy Zz

Open the book you are reading at the moment. Find 10 words starting with this letter and write them in cursive below

_____   _____

_____   _____

_____   _____

_____   _____

_____   _____

Sound [au]

Letter Combinations
OW

CROWN
DROWN
COW
NOW

___
___
___
___
___

[ou] — [au]

own — owl
bowl — brown
mow — pow

Letter Combinations
OU

OUT
DOUBT
CLOUD
LOUD

___
___
___
___
___

COMIC TIME

Create a pirate comic strip

Letter E

DRAW AS MANY THINGS THAT INCLUDE THE LETTER E AS YOU CAN!

CURSIVE WRITING

Aa Bb Cc Dd (Ee) Ff Gg

Hh Ii Jj Kk Ll Mm Nn

Oo Pp Qq Rr Ss Tt Uu

Vv Ww Xx Yy Zz

Open the book you are reading at the moment. Find 10 words starting with this letter and write them in cursive below

_____   _____

_____   _____

_____   _____

_____   _____

_____   _____

Sound [e]

Letter E in the closed syllable of the root	Letter Combinations EA	Letter E in the prefixes "EM" "EN"
BET SET ACCEPT ___ ___ ___ ___	BREAD DEAD HEAD ___ ___ ___ ___	ENJOY EMPLOY EMBRACE ___ ___ ___ ___

MAKE A FUNNY POEM WITH WORDS THAT HAVE AN EA LETTER COMBINATION

COLOR IN THE PICTURES AND FINISH THE WORDS WITH THIS LETTER

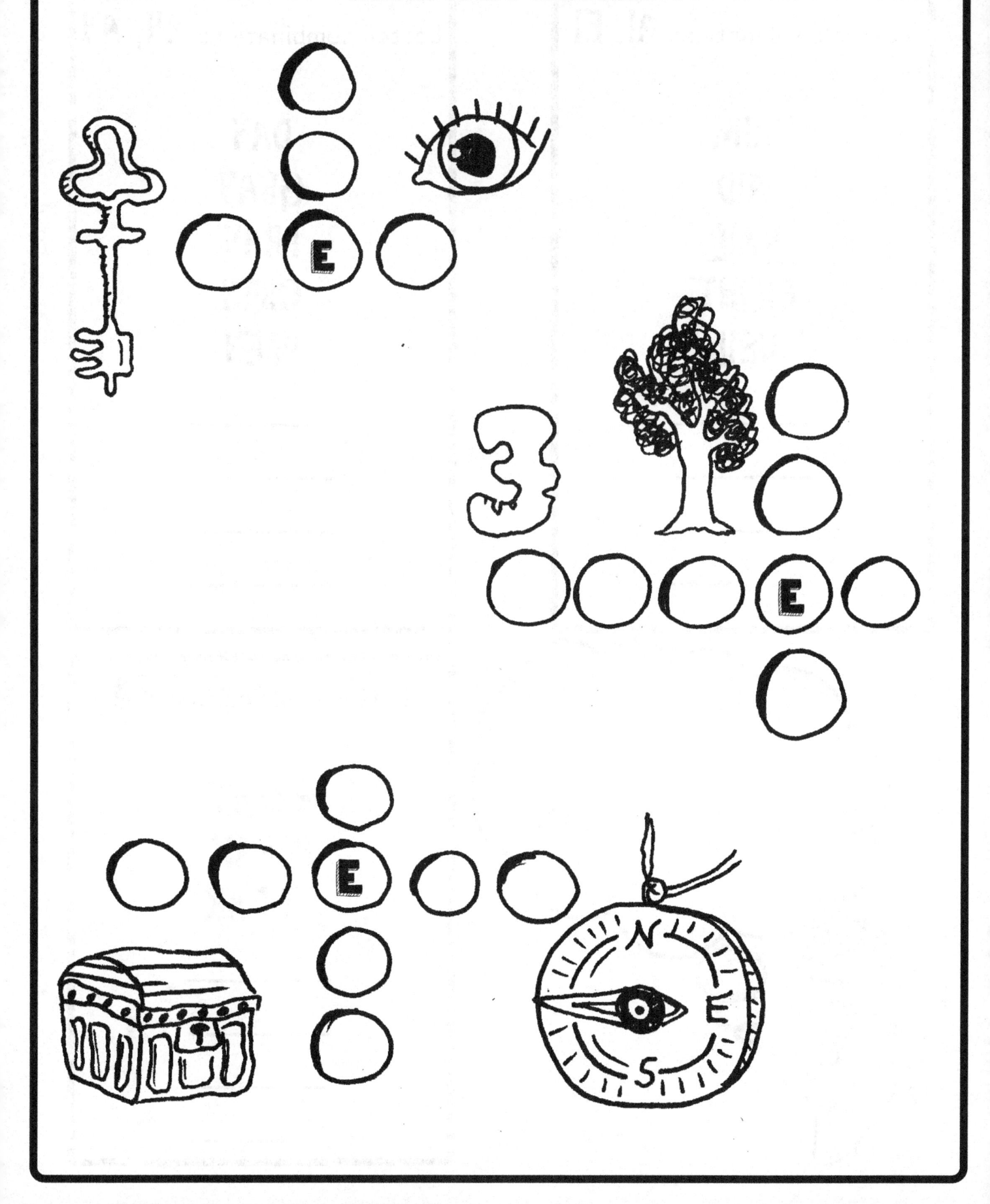

Sound [ei]

Letter combinations AI, EI

AIM
AID
SAIL
EIGHT
VEIL

_____
_____
_____
_____

Letter combinations AY, EY

DAY
GRAY
PRAY
OBEY
PREY

_____
_____
_____
_____

Letter combinations EA

GREAT
BREAK
STEAK

_____
_____
_____
_____

Sound [ei]

Letter A
in the open syllable of the root

KATE
LATE
PASTE
WASTE

_____
_____
_____
_____

Letter A
in the verbal suffix "ATE"

DECORATE
EDUCATE
CELEBRATE
CREATE

_____
_____
_____
_____

WRITE 3 FUNNY SENTENCES USING THE WORDS FROM THESE PAGES

1. _____
2. _____
3. _____

Letter I

DRAW AS MANY THINGS THAT START WITH LETTER I AS YOU CAN!

COLOR IN THE PICTURES AND FINISH THE WORDS WITH THIS LETTER

Sound [i]

Letter I
in the closed syllable of the root

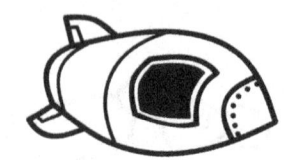

SIT
MISS
FINGER

___
___
___

Letter E
in some suffixes and endings

MADNESS
COUNTLESS
ROCKET
POCKET

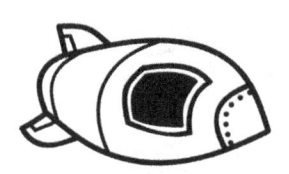

___
___
___

Letter Y
in the root

SYMBOL
HYMN
MYSTERY

___
___
___
___

Letter Y
in the suffix

LADY
FAMILY
BUSY
FUNNY

___
___
___
___

Sound [i]

Letter Combinations **IE**	Letter Combinations **EY**
ANNIE	HONEY
CARRIE	JOURNEY
KATIE	MONEY
_____	_____
_____	_____
_____	_____
_____	_____

MAKE UP SHORT FUNNY POEMS USING THE WORDS FROM THESE PAGES

Sound [i:]

Letter E
in the open syllable of the root

ME
SHE
PETE
___
___
___
___

Letter E
in the suffixes "ESE"

CHINESE
JAPANESE
___
___
___
___

Letter E
in the prefixes "pre, re"

REMOVE
PREPARE
___
___
___
___

Letter Combinations
IE, EI

BELIEVE
ACHIEVE
RECEIVE
DECEIVE
___
___
___

Letter Combinations
EE, EA

DEEP
SEE
SEA
TEA
___
___
___

CREATIVE WRITING

Write an interesting short story or a poem using as many words with this sound as you can and draw an illustration about it below

Title:
_____

_____
_____
_____
_____
_____
_____
_____
_____
_____
_____

MAKE AN ILLUSTRATION ABOUT IT!

Letter O

COLOR IN THE PICTURES AND FINISH THE WORDS WITH THIS LETTER

CURSIVE WRITING

Aa Bb Cc Dd Ee Ff Gg
Hh Ii Jj Kk Ll Mm Nn
Oo Pp Qq Rr Ss Tt Uu
Vv Ww Xx Yy Zz

Open the book you are reading at the moment. Find 10 words starting with this letter and write them in cursive below

_____   _____

_____   _____

_____   _____

_____   _____

_____   _____

Sound [O]

Letter Combinations
WA

WASH
WANT
SWAMP

___
___
___

Letter O

BORROW
SORROW
CLOCK
COFFEE

___
___
___

Letter Combinations
QUA

QUALITY
QUARANTINE
QUARREL

___
___
___

Sound [Oi]

Letter Combinations
OI

OIL
POISON
VOICE

___
___
___

Letter Combinations
OY

BOY
JOY
ANNOY

___
___
___

CREATIVE WRITING

Write an interesting short story or a poem using as many words with this sound as you can and draw an illustration about it below

Title:
_____

_____
_____
_____
_____
_____
_____
_____
_____
_____
_____

MAKE AN ILLUSTRATION ABOUT IT!

Sound [O:]

Letter Combinations	Letter Combinations
WA, WAR	ALL, AL
WARM	CALL
WATER	SALT
REWARD	CHALK
____	____
____	____
____	____
____	____

WRITE A SHORT FUNNY POEM USING THE WORDS FROM THESE PAGES

Letter Combinations
OR, ORE

TORN
FORM
SHORE

___
___
___
___

Letter Combinations
AW

DAWN
HAWK
AWFUL

___
___
___
___

Letter Combinations
AUGHT, OUGHT

CAUGHT
BROUGHT
SOUGHT

___
___
___
___

Letter Combinations
AU

CAUSE
PAUSE
HAUNT

___
___
___
___

Sound [OU]

Letter O
in the open syllable of the root

HOME
HOPE
MOMENT
TOTAL

___
___
___
___

Letter O
in the closed syllable of the root
Before consonant

COLD
OLD
GHOST

___
___
___
___

Letter O
in the prefixes "CO" and "PRO"

COWORKER
COORDINATE
PROHIBIT
PROGRAM

___
___
___
___

USE THIS SPACE FOR FUNNY DRAWINGS AND DOODLES

Letter Combinations OW	Letter O in the final position	Letter Combinations OA
ROW FLOW KNOW	HERO ZERO POTATO TOMATO	SOAK BOAT ROAST

WRITE A SHORT FUNNY POEM USING THE WORDS FROM THESE PAGES

Letter U

DRAW AS MANY THINGS THAT INCLUDE THE LETTER U AS YOU CAN!

COLOR IN THE PICTURES AND FINISH THE WORDS WITH THIS LETTER (YES, PIRATES WERE BAD)

CURSIVE WRITING

Aa Bb Cc Dd Ee Ff Gg
Hh Ii Jj Kk Ll Mm Nn
Oo Pp Qq Rr Ss Tt (Uu)
Vv Ww Xx Yy Zz

Open the book you are reading at the moment. Find 10 words starting with this letter and write them in cursive below

_____   _____

_____   _____

_____   _____

_____   _____

_____   _____

Sound [U:]

Letter Combinations OO

FOOD
MOON
TATTOO

___
___
___
___

Letter O

DO
TWO
WHO

___
___
___
___

Letter Combinations OU

GROUP
SOUP
WOUND

___
___
___
___

Letter Combinations EW

JEWEL
BLEW
CHEW

___
___
___
___

Letter Combinations UE

TRUE
BLUE
CLUE

___
___
___
___

Sound [U]

Letter Combinations OO	Letter U	Letter Combinations OU
BOOK	PUSH	SHOULD
COOK	BULLET	WOULD
HOOD	SUGAR	COULD

___

WRITE 3 FUNNY SENTENCES USING THE WORDS FROM THESE PAGES

1. _____

2. _____

3. _____

Sound [ɚ]

Letter Combinations
ER

HERB
PERSON
PAPER
BETTER

___
___
___

Letter Combinations
UR, IR

BURN
TURN
SIR
CIRCLE

___
___
___

Letter Combinations
OUR

JOURNAL
COURAGE
JOURNEY

___
___
___

Letter Combinations
OR

WORD
FAVOR
EFFORT

___
___
___

Letter Combinations
AR

DOLLAR
COLLAR
COWAR

_____
_____
_____
_____
_____

Letter Combinations
EAR

LEARN
EARTH
PEARL

_____
_____
_____
_____
_____

**WRITE A SHORT FUNNY POEM
USING THE WORDS FROM THESE PAGES**

NEUTRAL SOUND
[ə] [ʌ]

is the most common vowel sound of English.
It occurs in initial, medial, or final position in the root, prefix, and suffix under stress or unstressed.

Letter A	Letter O	Letter U
ABOUT	SON	DIFFICULT
SODA	LESSON	NUMBER
CENTRAL	FREEDOM	SUN
CINEMA	MONEY	MINUS
_____	_____	_____
_____	_____	_____
_____	_____	_____
_____	_____	_____

MAKE FUNNY DRAWINGS ABOUT THE WORDS ABOVE

Letter Combinations
OU

Letter I
TERRIBLE
POSSIBLE
FAMILY

___
___
___
___

ROUGH
TOUGH
TROUBLE
DOUBLE

___
___
___
___

Letter E
TOLERATE
GOLDEN
KITTEN

___
___
___
___

WRITE A SHORT STORY USING AS MANY OF THE SOUNDS ABOVE:

___
___
___
___
___
___
___
___
___

Letter Combination EA

SORT THE WORDS BELOW BY THE SOUNDS

sea, tea, flea, peace, beach, teach, lead, read, beak, peak, leak, freak, deal, meal, reveal, seal, steal, beam, cream, scream, team, bean, lean, clean, heap, leap, reap, please, treasure, measure, pleasure, release, increase, tease, meat, beat, heat, beneath, breathe, creature, leave, great, steak. head, header, lead, read, spread, thread, dread, tread, ready, instead, sweat, sweater, threat, threaten, breath, death, deaf, health, stealth, wealth, weather, leather, leak, freak, deal, meal, feather, treacherous, pleasant, jealous, bread, dead, dealt, meant, cleanse, weapon, heaven, heavy, breakfast, breast, break

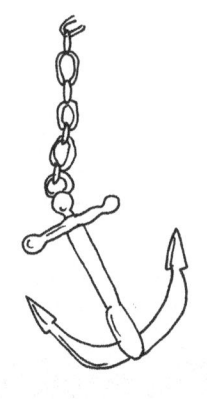

USE THE SPACE ABOVE TO DOODLE

SORT THE WORDS FROM THE PREVIOUS PAGE BY SOUND

[i:]	[e:]	[ei]
SEA	BREAD	BREAK
TEA	DEAD	

Letter coMbiNatioN OW

SORT THESE WORDS BY THE SOUNDS AND WRITE THEM ON THE LIST ON THE NEXT PAGE

follow, hollow, borrow, narrow, window, yellow, now, how, cow, row, bow, brow, allow, crowd, powder, owl, fowl, howl, down, gown, town, know, low, show, row, bow, clown, brown, drown, crown, browse, browser, towel, bowel, vowel, mow, owe, tow, crow, grow, throw, flower, power, tower, blow, flow, slow, bowl, own, blown, flown, grown, shown, thrown, growth, coward, Howard

USE THE SPACE ABOVE TO DOODLE

[oʊ]	[aʊ]
FOLLOW	CROWD
HOLLOW	ALLOW

THE -S/ES ENDING OF NOUNS

WRITE AS MANY PLURAL NOUNS IN THE BUBBLE BELOW AS YOU CAN

apples   FISHES   KITES

SORT THEM BY THE SOUNDS

[S]   [Z]   [IZ]
KITES   APPLES   FISHES

_____   _____   _____
_____   _____   _____
_____   _____   _____
_____   _____   _____

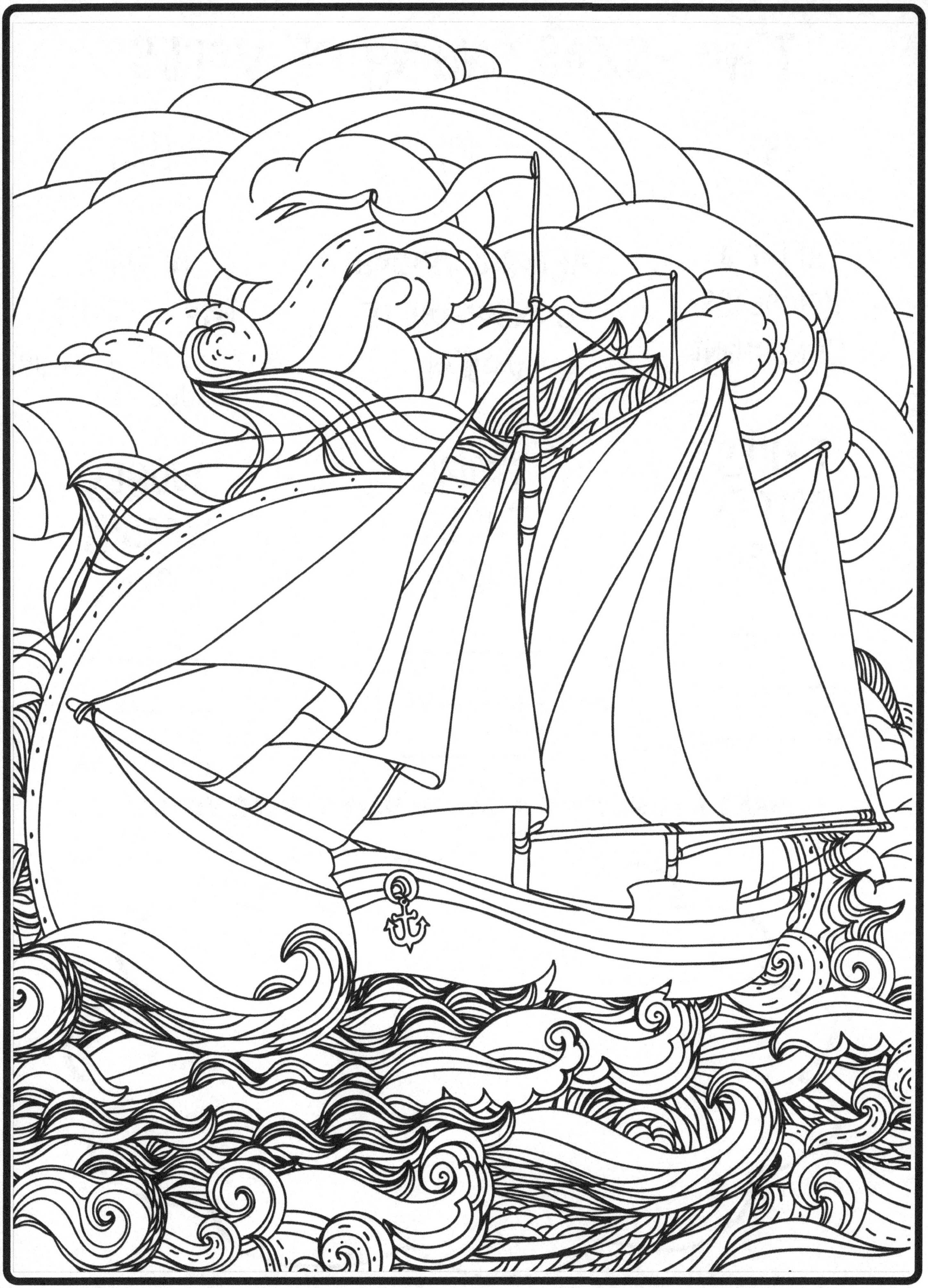

The -s/es ending of verbs

[S]	[Z]	[IZ]
After a voiceless consonant	After a voiced consonant or vowel	After the letters s, z, x, ch, tch, ge, dge, sh
TAKES WRITES BITES	SWIMS FALLS CRIES	JUDGES WASHES LOSES
___ ___ ___	___ ___ ___	___ ___ ___

MAKE A FUNNY POEM BELOW USING THESE WORDS

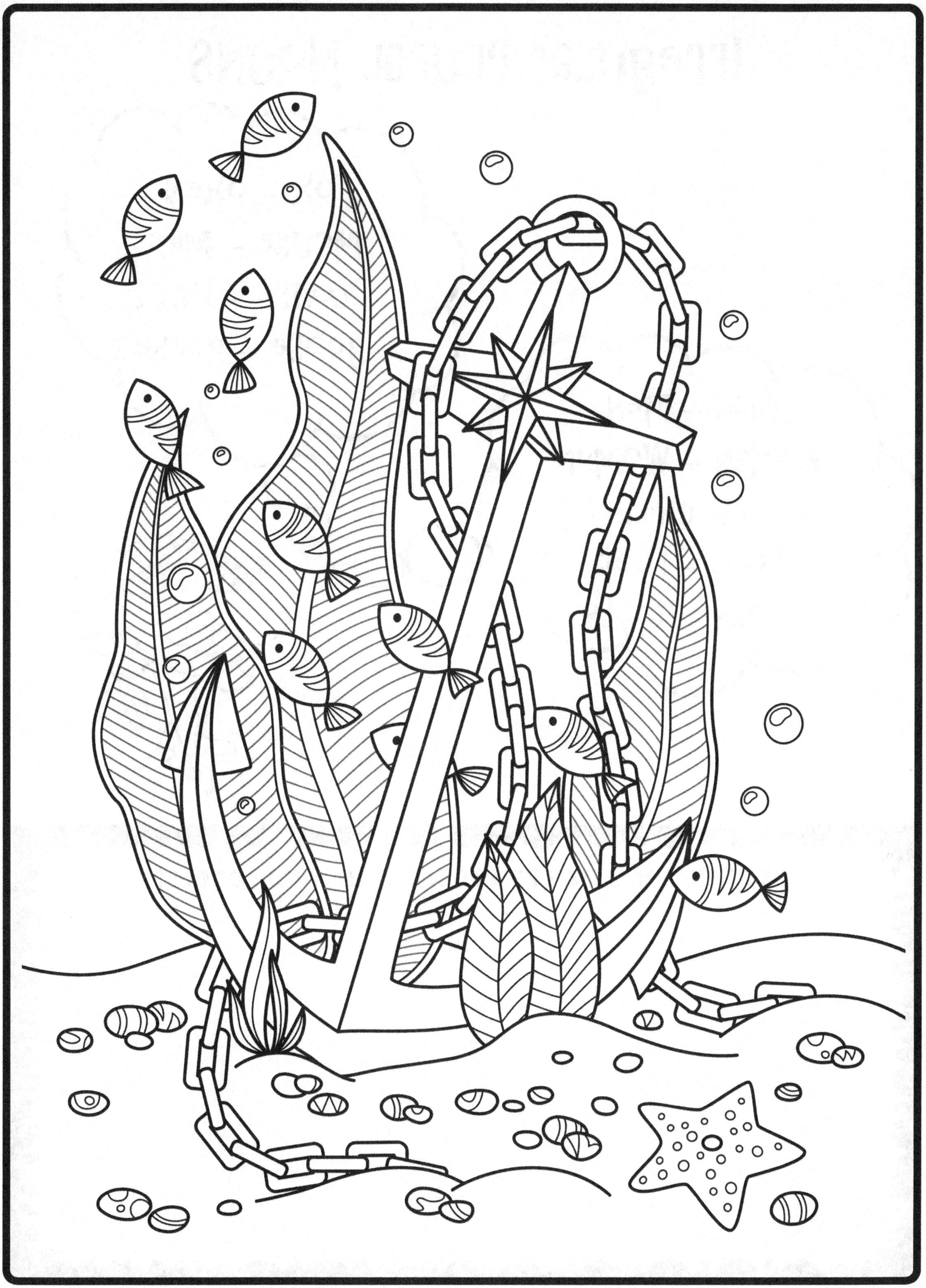

Irregular Plural Nouns

Ox – Oxen
Mouse – Mice
Louse – Lice
Goose – Geese

Man – Men
Woman – Women
Child – Children
Foot – Feet
Tooth – Teeth

USE THIS SPACE FOR FUNNY DRAWINGS AND DOODLES

The Same Singular and Plural NOUN Form

- SHEEP
- FISH
- BISON
- MEANS
- DOZEN
- SWINE
- SERIES
- ALMS
- CROSSROADS
- AIRCRAFT

NOUNS ONLY IN PLURAL

- JEANS
- TROUSERS
- PANTS
- SHORTS
- TIGHTS
- PAJAMAS
- SCISSORS
- PLIERS

WRITE TWO FUNNY SENTENCES USING THE WORDS FROM THESE PAGES

1. _____

2. _____

ENGLISH HOMONYMS

The same pronunciation, different meaning

AIR – HEIR
BUY – BY – BYE
CEREAL – SERIAL
DEAR – DEER
TOO – TWO

_____

_____

_____

_____

WRITE 3 FUNNY SENTENCES USING HOMONYMS

1. _____

2. _____

3. _____

The same spelling, different pronunciation and meaning

TEAR [tiər] – TEAR [teər]
BOW [bau] – BOW [bau]
DESERT ['dezərt] – DESSERT [di'zərt]

_____

_____

_____

_____

DRAW SOME OF THESE WORDS! WHAT DO THEY MEAN?

SUFFIXES
NOUNS

-HOOD
Parenthood
_____
_____
_____

-DOM
Kingdom
_____
_____
_____
_____

-MENT
Basement
_____
_____
_____

-NESS
Kindness
_____
_____
_____

Creative Writing

Write a short story using as many of these words as you can and draw an illustration about it below

Title:
_____

NOUNS

-SHIP
Worship
_____
_____
_____
_____

-SION
Compassion
_____
_____
_____
_____

-TH
Health
_____
_____
_____
_____

-TION
Potion
_____
_____
_____
_____

-Ty
Ability
_____
_____
_____

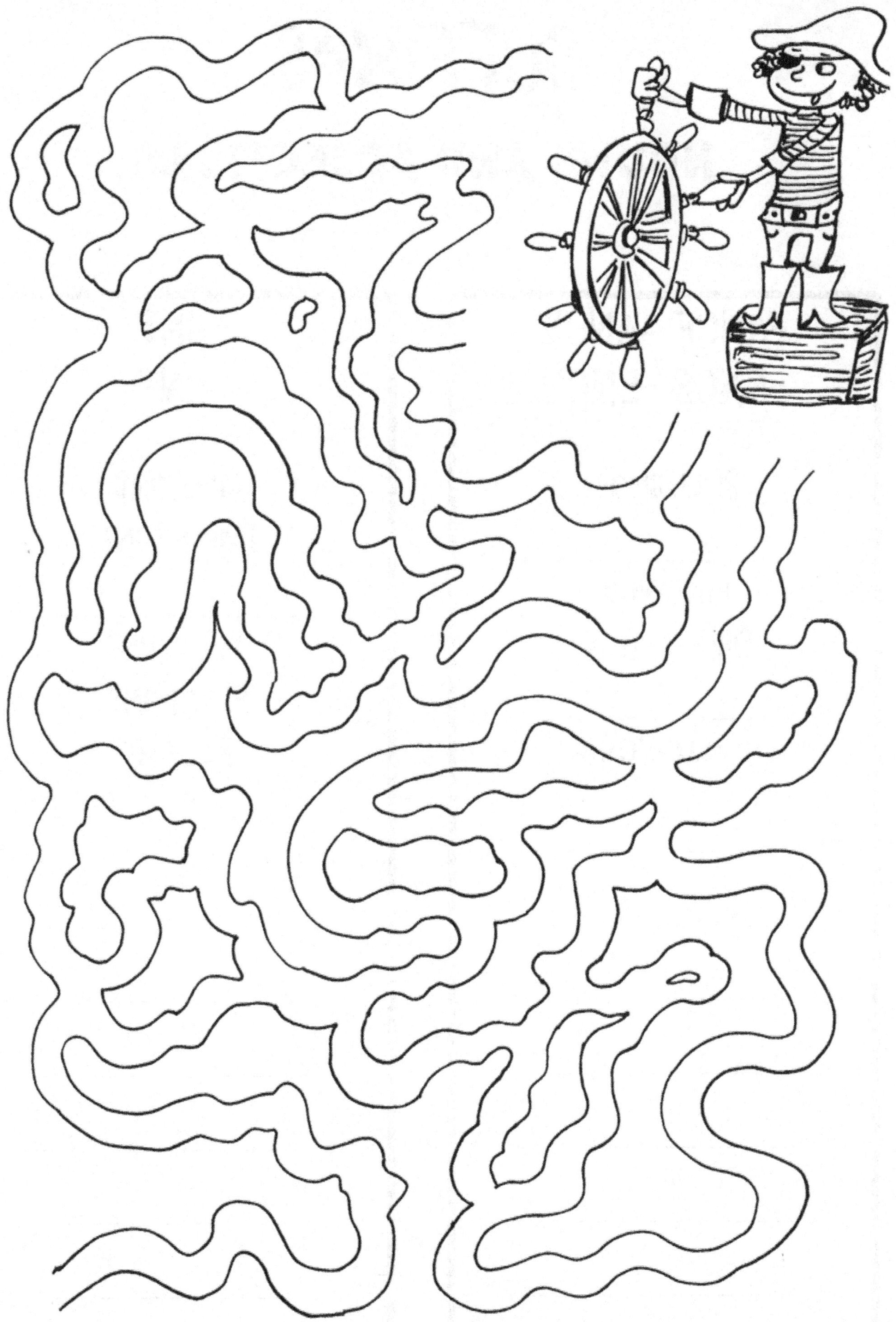

SUFFIXES
NOUNS AND ADJECTIVES

-ANCE -ANCY
-ENCE -ENCY

Brilliance
___
Patience
Difference
___
Fluency
___
___
___
___
___
___
___

-ANT
-ENT

Brilliant
Important
___
Different
Pregnant
Fluent
___
___
___
___
___
___
___

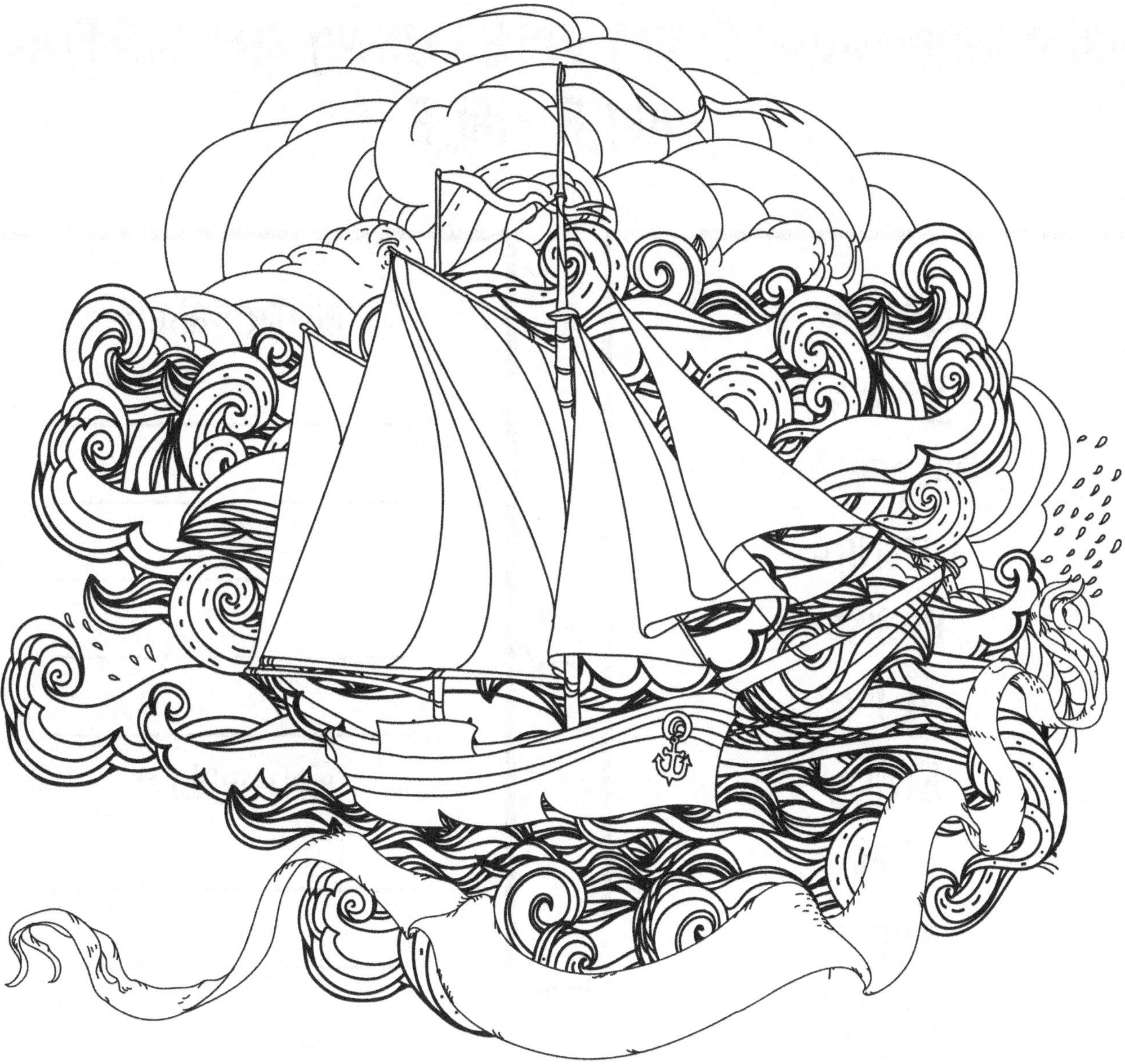

SUFFIXES
ADJECTIVES

Make adjectives from verbs using the suffixes -ABLE -IBLE

Notice	Noticeable
Sense	
Response	
Change	
Resist	
Try	
Enjoy	Enjoyable
Eat	
Agree	
Accept	
respect	

Make adjectives from nouns using the suffix -ful

Beauty	Beautiful
Care	_____
Faith	_____
Trust	_____
Friend	_____
Joy	_____
Taste	_____
Peace	_____
Delight	_____
Help	_____
Fruit	Fruitful
_____	_____

WRITE TWO SENTENCES USING THE WORDS FROM THESE PAGES

1. _____

2. _____

SUFFIXES
ADJECTIVES

-OUS
Dangerous
_____
_____
_____
_____

-IVE
Active
_____
_____
_____
_____
_____
_____

-Y
Funny
_____
_____
_____
_____

-IC
Fantastic
_____
_____
_____
_____

Make adjectives from nouns using the suffix -LESS

Self	Selfless
Blame	_____
Child	_____
Pain	_____
Noise	_____
Hope	_____
Head	_____
Power	_____
Limit	_____
End	Endless

WRITE A SHORT STORY USING THE WORDS ABOVE:

_____
_____
_____
_____
_____
_____
_____

SUFFIXES
ADJECTIVES

-ED

Amazed
Bored
_____
_____
_____
_____
_____
_____
_____

-ING

Amazing
_____
_____
_____
_____

Tiring
Exhausting
Annoying
_____
_____

WHAT DIFFERENCE DO THESE SUFFIXES MAKE IN MEANING?

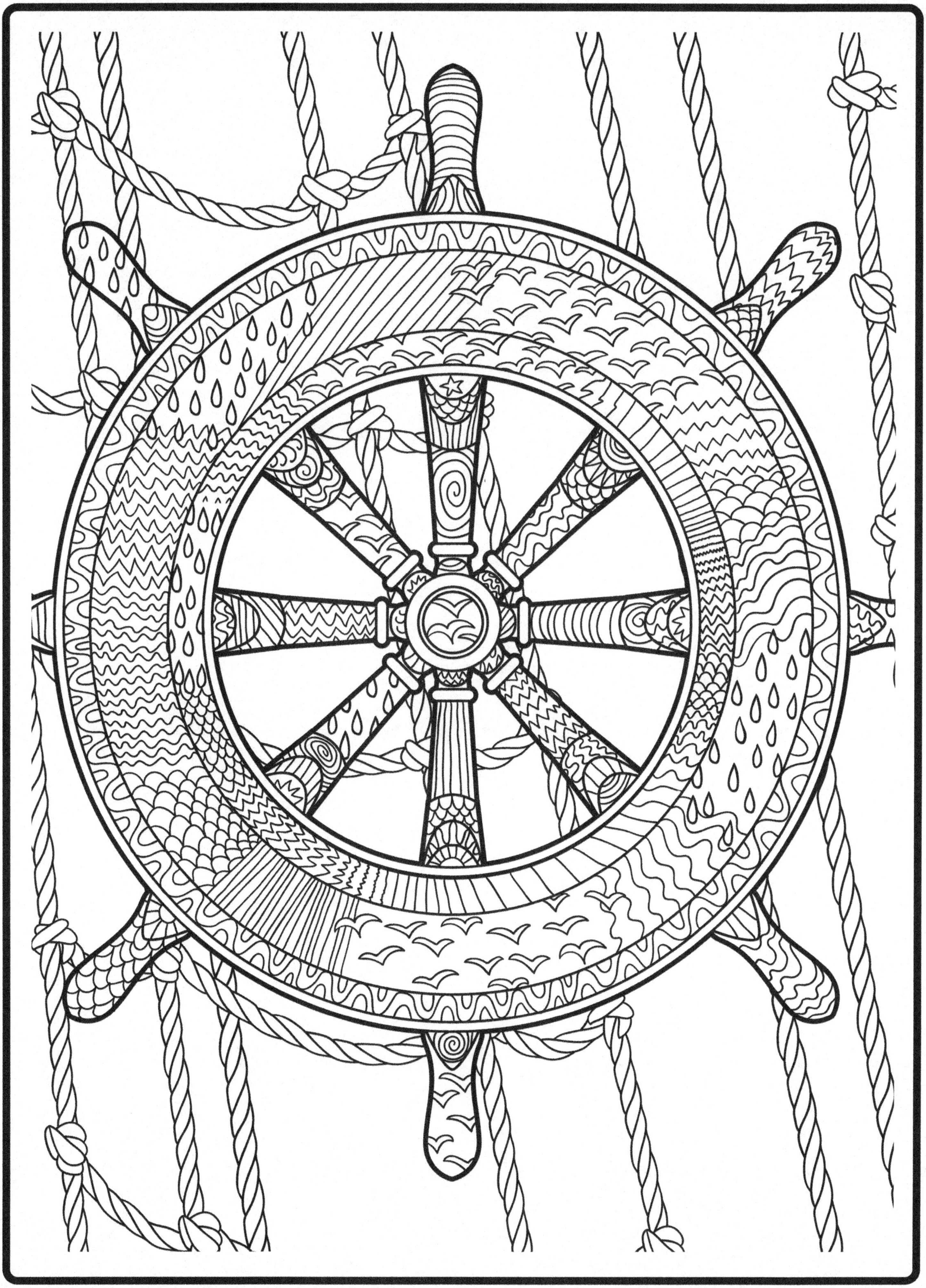

What Is Fun-Schooling?

Fun-schooling is a one-of-a-kind way to learn. It is tapping into kids interests while covering all the major subjects. Fun-schooling is for creative learners, students with learning disabilities, gifted students, and everyone in between. It's a way for students to learn without the stress, pressure, and boredom of other methods. We started out creating materials for our children. Then friends and family wanted to try it out. Before we knew it, Fun-schooling with Thinking Tree Books was born!

Fun-Schooling With Thinking Tree Books

Copyright Information

Thinking Tree Fun-Schooling Books, and electronic printable downloads are for home and family use only. You may make copies of these materials for only the children in your household.

All other uses of this material must be permitted in writing by Thinking Tree LLC. It is a violation of copyright law to distribute the electronic files or make copies for your friends, associates or students without. For information on using these materials for businesses, co-ops, summer camps, day camps, daycare, afterschool program, churches, or schools please contact us for licensing.

Contact Us:

The Thinking Tree LLC

+1 (USA) 317.622.8852

info@funschooling.com

THE THINKING TREE

FunSchooling.com

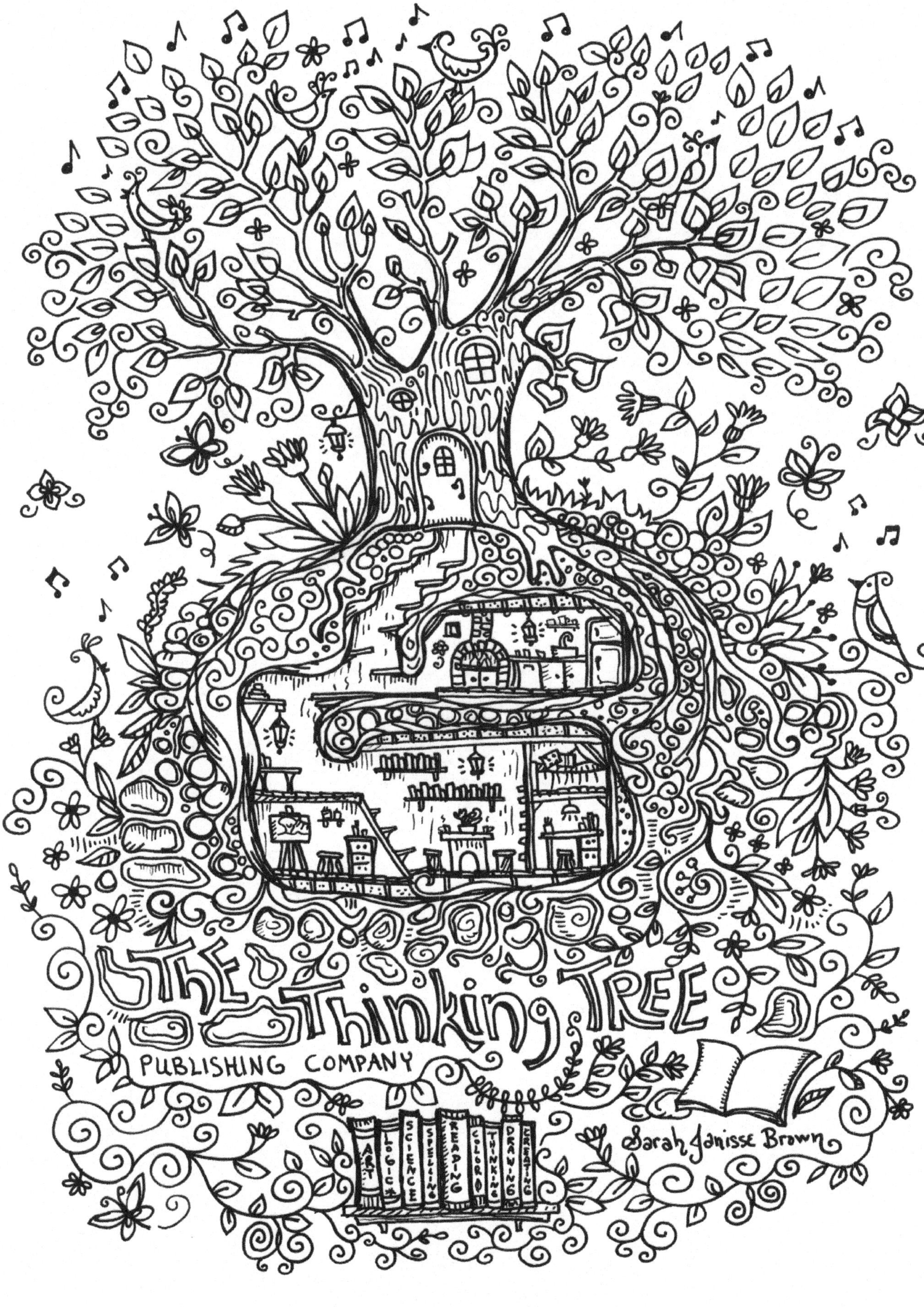

Made in the USA
Columbia, SC
20 August 2025